the orphaned generation

THE FATHER'S HEART FOR CONNECTING YOUTH AND YOUNG ADULTS TO YOUR CHURCH

scott wilcher

Published by The Upstream Project
1108 Crystalwood Circle
Chesapeake, VA 23320

www.scottwilcher.com

Printed in the United States of America

Cover Art by Levi Bethune

Illustrations by Ann Wilcher

the orphaned generation

THE FATHER'S HEART FOR CONNECTING
YOUTH AND YOUNG ADULTS
TO YOUR CHURCH

The Orphaned Generation

For Michele

There's not enough space to explain
the medal you deserve—though you would refuse it,
which explains so much of why you deserve it.
I am grateful.

The Orphaned Generation

Contents

The Orphaned Generation

About This Book

Who Should Read This Book?

This book is written for adult Christians whose churches are struggling to attract and/or keep young people.

What's the Big Idea?

God designed us to think about abstract things using concrete pictures. When our minds are renewed to approach more closely the mind of Christ, those pictures change, and then our behavior toward young people changes.

This book identifies our mental pictures and offers renewed images in four domains: the Gospel, young people, adult relationships to young people, and the Church. Those renewed pictures will allow you and your church to see young people with fresh eyes, love them better, and help them become lifelong disciples of Jesus Christ.

Preface

T his book is not a tightrope. It's not calling Christians to walk a particular way or else face the danger of a misstep. This book is a springboard, intended to send each reader forward into deeper relationships with the Father and His Church—and to launch you with enthusiasm and without fear toward young people in and around your church.

It's intended to renew your thinking and provoke discussion in and between churches and to change lives from the inside out. Jesus' prayer in John 17 was that we would be one, as He was one with the Father. I want to unite the Church to clear a common hurdle—growing the next generation into lifelong followers of Jesus Christ.

Thanks for reading. I welcome your comments, thoughts, and questions at scottwilcher.com.

A Story

I don't cuss much, but late one Friday night on my way home from consulting with a church, I pulled in to get gas at a pump behind a van filled with teenagers. They were from a church in the western part of Virginia, presumably on their way to the beach just twenty minutes away from the gas station. The tired driver (probably the youth pastor judging by his goatee, T-shirt, and flip-flops) was pumping gas, leaning heavily against the van. He seemed to savor the solitude outside the noisy vehicle, so I didn't bother him.

I had been a youth pastor for many years and knew those moments of solitude were precious, so I pumped my gas, smiling, listening to the happy chatter of teenagers carting armloads of sugary snacks. I thought back on the Sarahs, Michaels, and Hannahs I'd taken on retreats and mission trips all over the world while we listened to soundtracks that started with Larry Norman when I was a kid and moved through the Second Chapter of Acts, Keith Green, Amy Grant, Michael W. Smith, Five Iron Frenzy, GRITS, Toby Mac, and a hundred others.

When his pump clunked to a stop, I snapped back to the present. The driver replaced the pump handle and the gas cap, grabbed his receipt (some church bookkeeper would be very happy), and he herded the stragglers aboard and climbed in.

As the van started to pull away, the teenage passengers pressed to the back windows and looked at me with conspiring smiles. I heard one counting and at three,

they all yelled in singsong fashion, "Jesus loves you!"
Then they cheered and laughed as the van moved off,
clapping and high-fiving to celebrate their sharing of
God's love for me.

Again, I don't cuss much, but that night I reacted.
Sudden heat rose in me. I breathed in sharply; my chin
lifted, and I was poised to shout mean, nasty things after
them.

But I stopped and just stood there, watching as their
van pulled out onto Battlefield Boulevard and took the on-
ramp toward the beach. In a moment I mumbled some
choice words to myself, then got in my car wondering,
"Where in the world had that reaction come from?"

Certainly I am a sinner who needs to be reminded of
the love of Christ, but why was I so angry? Was I just
tired? Was I harboring some hidden resentment? Perhaps
I was wounded that they failed to see the glow of the
anointing on my life and ministry. Perhaps I should just
put a fish on my car. Or perhaps I had no anointing at all!
Perhaps it was because they clearly did not have their
seatbelts on.

At first I wasn't sure. It was an odd moment, but as I
neared my house the answer became clear to me. The

moment at the pump was a gift designed by God just for me—I got to see something I needed to see and feel something I needed to feel: Those kids on that van wanted me to be in relationship with Jesus, but they didn't care to be in relationship with *me*.

Their message of God's love to me felt empty, or worse, taunting—like scraps they'd thrown at a stray dog. As they drove off, I felt alone, more alone than moments before. I felt abandoned there at the gas pumps, as they drove away cheerful . . . together in their van. I didn't like the feeling. I blamed it on them, and I resented them for it.

I have worked with young people and their families my entire adult life (30+ years). These days I am pressing for the adult Christians to move toward the young people in discipling relationships, but this night was different. The tables were turned on me. I got a taste of how a young person (or anybody) feels when the people of the Church share the love of Christ from a distance, or worse, as we move away from them.

I came to faith in Jesus in the early 1970s. It was the era when the Living Bible had just come out, and we all covered our copies in denim. It was the era when Billy Graham Crusades were effective for reaching the lost. It was an era when it was common to hear stories like that of my friend Joe, who was walking down a sidewalk in Charlotte, NC. A city bus pulled up near him, and, when the doors opened, a woman stepped off the bus, handed Joe a cartoon tract about a guy who faced judgment after his unexpected death in a car wreck. She climbed back on the bus and was gone, but by the time Joe reached the end of the block, he prayed the prayer on the back of the tract and became a Christian.

But it's not the 70s anymore. It's a new era, a new season in God's Kingdom and in the culture. The mindset of most young people has changed. They don't trust TV evangelists. They don't trust strangers who speak from pulpits. They don't believe bumper stickers . . . or tracts found on the toilet paper dispenser in a public bathroom. They know when they are being sold something, and they don't want you to convince them something is beneficial for their lives, unless the evidence is obvious in your life.

If we toss the Gospel to them from a distance, we simply reinforce their perception that we are not interested in them at all, that they are the outsiders, not wanted in our van, in our lives, or in our churches.

I wrote this book to aid the renewal of our minds to more closely reflect the mind of Christ. I wrote this book to change the way the Church shares the love of Christ with one another and with outsiders, especially with young people in and around the church. I've seen changes in every church where I have preached its content, and I pray for you that it changes your heart and renews your mind. More than that, I pray God then uses you and your church to reach a generation of young people that feels abandoned by the adults in their lives.

The Opportunity Right Beside Us

Mr. Harding's seat was taken—the aisle seat on the seventh pew from the front, right side. It was his seat nearly every Sunday for over thirty years, the pew where he'd sat with his wife and kids. But his kids had grown up and moved away. And since his wife had died three years ago, he'd sat alone.

Over those thirty years Mr. Harding watched the church change. The faces changed. The service changed. The music changed. The pastor changed. Everything changed.

Except Mr. Harding's seat.

So now he stood in the center aisle beside the seventh pew, right side, trying to figure out what to do about the dark-haired kid who sat slumped in his seat.

David had come to church looking for his friend and some food. The friend was a classmate who had invited him to come to this church a couple of weeks ago. He had assured David he was welcome anytime and that there would be free doughnuts and muffins. David had blown off the invitation, but after last night he reconsidered. His stepfather had come home drunk again. The shouting started, and David knew better than to get involved. He'd learned that the hard way, so he'd left and spent the night on a neighbor's deck in a padded lounge chair, sleeping some, but mostly looking at the stars and wondering about his future. This morning all the deep thinking was done, and David was hungry.

He walked to the church, and an older gentleman showed him where the doughnuts were and poured him a cup of weak coffee that looked like tea. David stood alone and ate two doughnuts, watching the people arrive. They were mostly older folks who seemed harmless enough. David had been in a church for weddings and a couple of funerals, so he decided to stay for the service. He was hoping to see his friend from school, but mostly he was just curious.

Two men in dark suits stood guarding the doors. One was talking about his vacation plans; the other listened and nodded. When David slipped between them, the silent man handed him a program and nodded. The other man kept talking. David moved up the center aisle and at the seventh pew from the front, right side, he sat down.

A few moments later, David became aware that someone was standing in the aisle. He turned. An old man was looking down at him. In one hand the man held a program in front of him like a shield. With his other hand, he patted his lips nervously. His face seemed sad, but in his eyes David recognized disapproval. He'd seen it often in other adult faces. David turned back toward the front and ignored him as long as he could. Finally, he turned and said, "Can I help you?" sounding a little meaner than he intended.

"Uh . . . that's my seat," the old man said flatly.

David grunted and slid wearily to his right, regretting that he came here at all. Mr. Harding claimed his seat, and the two of them sat—only a few feet apart, but the gap between them felt huge. They both sat silently— a lonely older man beside a frightened teen who was losing hope that he'd ever find his way. This morning each was unaware of the needs of the other; each was blind to the glorious opportunity orchestrated just for them . . . and for the church.

Inertia

Mr. Harding's story may be our story. What happened to him on a Sunday morning probably happens in our lives every week at church, at work, or at home. God disrupts the comfortable routine of our lives with an opportunity to reach out to a younger person who needs some healthy influence in his life.[1]

There are Davids all around us. Many of us think they are the youth pastor's responsibility. That thinking will kill your church. Young people are leaving our churches because of that thinking, and those outside the church are not reached at all, because of that thinking.

---

[1] For convenience and clarity throughout this book, I will avoid the use of "his/her" and use the singular masculine pronouns (he or his) to represent either gender.

Though most people come to faith before they are 18 years old, the traditional model of youth ministry is no longer working in most churches. It no longer attracts significant numbers of unchurched teens into relationship with Jesus. Nor does it keep the active kids in the church into adulthood. Many studies demonstrate that young people who were active in a church as children are leaving in significant numbers by the age of 25. Most American studies put the range between seventy and almost ninety percent. The future of the church is bleak—unless we implement changes.

But we move through our lives in a particular direction for particular reasons at a particular speed, reluctant to change unless acted upon by some force, some outside interference. In physics it's called inertia—the resistance of any object to change its state of motion. It's a principle that can also apply figuratively to our movement through life and our reluctance to change our thinking and our behaviors.

Inertia affects churches as well. The collective inertia of the individuals in your church tends to cause it to continue in a particular direction at a constant speed, unless acted on by an outside force. Most of us think the staff and lay leadership of our church alone should be that force, but that thinking will kill your church. In most churches, leaders struggle to manage the amount of change they currently face. They are reluctant to initiate more or faster changes that might attract young people for fear of further alienating the older members.

Consequently, the Church is losing people on both ends of the demographic: Young people are wandering off, and older members are becoming less active or pass away.

If churches intend to reach and keep the next generation as lifelong disciples of Jesus Christ, their members must renew the way they think about young people, the role of adults in their lives, and the role of the Church. Simply commanding young people to "stay in church" is not enough force to change the direction of their lives. In the same way, commanding adult congregations to "reach out to young people" is not enough to change the trajectory of their lives. We must look deeper. We need to answer three questions:

1. Why are young people leaving our church?
2. Why do adults in our church struggle to reach out to them effectively?
3. What must we do to reach and keep them?

In coming chapters, we'll learn answers to those questions, but knowledge alone is not the solution. There must be a renewal of our minds that presses us toward something more than just knowledge. We need fresh eyes to see the Davids all around us—in our churches, neighborhoods, and workplaces—the young men and women who have the potential to be heroes in the faith, but lack the guidance to reach their destinies. Paul writes to the church in Corinth, *"We have the mind of Christ."* (2:16) The mind behind your eyes can begin to more fully reflect His mind. If your church is to reach young people, it must.

Will you pray this prayer?

Father, if I am to be Your follower, my mind must become more like the mind of Christ. Will You use the content of this book in that process? Will You open my heart and mind to find Your message as I read it? Will You show me where my mind needs renewing?

Part One:
Why Are They Leaving?

1

Why Are Young People Leaving?

My friend Barry Taylor called hundreds of young people to ask them why they left active participation in their churches. Barry compiled their responses and summarized them in three simple statements he heard over and over:

"They don't want me."

"They don't trust me."

"They lied to me."

My experience in youth ministry and church consulting affirms these responses are accurate. So let's unpack each one, giving full credit to Barry for the effort and the clarity he offered.

2

They Don't Want Me!

Young people won't stay in a community if they don't feel wanted. Consider a normal kid in a typical church: We'll call him Norm. Norm attended an age-appropriate Sunday school class and was active in an excellent youth ministry that he said, "felt like family."

In June, Norm and his classmates are being honored on Graduation Sunday, where the pastor explains they are now part of the adult church. Norm wonders, "Why would I get involved with the adult church?"

He's been separated from it for years, and he has no relationships with it. Furthermore, the adults constantly complain about the youth group's behavior or the mess they leave. Why would Norm join a group that's always been critical of his current group that feels like a family?

Simultaneously, Norm is discouraged from continuing with the youth community. He's told he's a graduate now. His parents suggest that he get involved in the young adult ministry, but it feels awkward to him. The group started as a college group ten years ago, and its members stayed together, so most of the members are nearing thirty years old. They're nice people who told Norm he was welcome to come, which is more than the older adults have done. But he feels too young for the group, and he thinks they were just being polite.

Church programming has pressed Norm into a relational vacuum between communities. Cut off from the youth group and feeling unwanted by the adult church, Norm does the reasonable thing—he wanders off. He doesn't leave suddenly. He's not angry; he's sad. With each visit, he's reminded that his church is not what it used to be. That persistent peck of disappointment makes his heart raw. He feels less motivated to attend. Eventually, Norm avoids his church, except on special occasions, but if no one at those events makes it clear that he is wanted, Norm leaves convinced that his perceptions are accurate: "They don't want me!"

Notice that the church is not just losing Norm. It's losing a cluster of friends around Norm as well. That cluster of friends may feel free to visit some of the "hotter" churches that try to reach people their age, but if they don't connect there, they will most likely end their active participation in a church.

Young people must feel genuinely wanted by your church if they are to stay.

3

They Don't Trust Me!

Stephen doesn't feel trusted. He'll be a graphic designer one day, but right now he's the nearly invisible young man sitting alone in an aging church. His friends have gone off to college, but, like more and more students, he has chosen to attend the local community college before transferring to another school. He sits cringing at the projected slides of misspelled song lyrics and hastily-made sermon outlines on stock backgrounds.

He cringes because he cares. He volunteered to help, but the folks who prepare the slides seemed offended when he suggested he could make them look better, telling him, "They're good enough. We're not trying to be slick in our presentation. Besides, it's easier if we handle it the way we've been doing it."

And with that Stephen learned, not only was he not wanted, he was not trusted. He won't stay there much longer. He's not rebellious; he's just reasonable. Why would he stay where he is not trusted? Why would we expect him to be willing to simply sit there passively and not contribute his gifts to the group? He may visit other churches soon, but he may fear they'll all treat him the same way.

Clearly, the people who sent Stephen that message

didn't intend it as a brush-off. They had reasons: the desire to remain undisturbed; the lack of energy to train a new person; or their fear of losing status or position, etc. But usually people carry the perception that it would be a burden on Stephen to take on responsibility. They're trying to be "nice." If Stephen were bolder, he would have pressed harder and insisted, but he's trying to be "nice" as well.

Young people in your church and community need to be needed. They are not content to sit passively and watch people do church up front. They want to own a part of it. They hope for a job, a way to contribute beyond just showing up. They are lumpy with undiscovered gifts and talents.

The wise church will encourage young people to unwrap those gifts and try them out. They don't need to preach the sermon, but they need to help somehow, to feel trusted with ownership of some part of the church.

Imagine how differently Stephen would feel if someone asked him to help, told him not simply that he was wanted, (which would be great!) but that he was

NEEDED, that the church needed his gifts in order to accomplish the history-making vision God had for it. Stephen would not wander off so easily from that community.

4

They Lied to Me!

Monica (not her real name) came to me after I finished one of my teachings at a weeklong retreat for three churches at Waterside, a wonderful camp in the mountains of Virginia. The week was going well, and I expected her to say, "Thanks for your message."

But she caught me off guard, when she asked, "Where is God? Why did He leave me?"

I asked her to explain a bit more and in her answer she said, "When Jesus is in your heart, you'll always be joyful. I don't feel joyful at all. So Jesus is not with me anymore."

Somebody told Monica a lie. They didn't mean to hurt her. They didn't mean to confuse her and cause her to doubt, but when well-meaning people teach a children's Gospel to young adults, the message kids hear sounds like—

"Come to Jesus; He'll change you so that you never want to sin . . . ever."

'Come to Jesus; He'll give you joy, you'll never be sad or angry . . . ever."

"Come to Jesus; He'll be your best friend, you'll never feel lonely or rejected . . . ever."

"Come to Jesus; He'll take all your problems. Just

set them at the foot of the cross."

Those statements are not biblically sound, but many young people (and old people) see the Christian life that way. If we teach our young people to expect Jesus to make it all better, and it's not all better, they get confused. Throw in the moral failure of a church leader, and/or the divorce of their Christian parents, and our young people will begin to grow embittered toward God, while the choir sings, *"Every day with Jesus is sweeter than the day before . . ."*

Apparently the whole choir believed it, so Monica alternated between resenting them for their faith and being ashamed of herself for her lack of it. By the time we talked, she was done playing nice.

Teaching the Truth

We must teach our young people that we share in the resurrection of Christ, but we also share in the suffering of Christ. We must teach them that God is willing to let us experience the valleys of trials and the spiritual deserts to build in us the enduring character of Christ.

The selling point of Christianity is not an easier life followed by entrance to heaven. The selling point is restored relationship with the Father and His presence in our lives no matter what may come, even death. Young people do not shrink from those hard aspects of a Gospel that requires sacrificial love. They want to do something hard, even dangerous, with their lives. Churches damage the faith of young converts when they try to minimize the sacrifice required of the Christian, when they tell kids just to be polite, reverent, and moral.

According to the research, our methods of discipleship have produced a "moralistic, therapeutic deism"[2] in many churched young people. In other words: They believe that God is out there watching, so be good, but His real purpose is to make your life better.

Yet, the contrasting reality of the Gospel is *"take up your cross," "lay down your life,"* and *"you may have had to suffer grief in all kinds of trials. These have come so that your faith—of greater worth than gold, which perishes even though refined by fire—may be proved genuine and may result in praise, glory, and honor when Jesus Christ is revealed."* (1 Peter 1:6b-7)

Those trials are not the absence of blessing. Our life in Christ is a blessing, but blessings come in some uncomfortable forms: Mary is called *"blessed among women,"* so she gets to be pregnant out of wedlock in a culture where women like that were stoned.

When our young people are taught something less than the whole truth, we rob them of that full-orbed perspective and may owe them an apology for it.

---

[2] Smith, Christian; Melinda Lundquist Denton (2005). Soul Searching: the religious and spiritual lives of American teenagers. Oxford University Press.

5

The Fullness of Hope

Yes, young people are leaving the Church in startling numbers, but I'm not trying to drain your hope or instill fear. I'm not Chicken Little crying, "The sky is falling!" I'm a rooster crowing, "Wake up!" to their departure, and, in that crowing, my message is, "We have great hope!"

Our Father's not wringing His hands, fretting over young people, confused about the decay of the family. He's not fearful of Post-Modern thought and the rise of technology. He is Lord of all.

Further, my intent is not to make adults feel guilty or shamed. My intent is that the Church love well and cast off guilt and fear. The dark gap between the generations is an opportunity for the Church to shine.

Like Mr. Harding, we sit beside an opportunity orchestrated by God, but we must uncover the reasons we behave as we currently do. Why do we remain unmoved and silent? Why are we reluctant to share our faith with them? Why are we scared to reach out to them? The answers to those questions in the coming chapters will help us see what God is doing in these times, and perhaps learn what we should be doing to join Him.

If we know three reasons why young people are

leaving the Church, then the next question is, "How do we reach and keep them?"

The answers seem simple enough:

Want them.

Trust them.

Tell them the truth.

But making that happen is not so simple. As modern church people, we tend to look for organizational solutions. Organizational efforts aren't without some value, but they'll fall short, unless there is a heart change in the congregation or in a portion of the congregation. Even if that portion is just one person (you, for instance) in the beginning, it is enough. It will grow, but it must start in our hearts and minds, not in a committee.

The solution is not organizational; it is relational. The most powerful retainer of young people in a church is not a program. It is a loving network of family, peer, AND adult relationships that are valuable, relevant, and safe. The only way a young person would leave such a community is through a significant life change (i.e., college plans or job availability) or a call to do something greater for the Kingdom, and that's not leaving, that's sending out.

But that network of relationships will not happen for young people until the adults in the Church begin to think differently, and, in time, behave differently toward them. That requires that our minds be renewed to reflect more closely the mind of Christ Jesus.

Part Two:
Thinking in Pictures

6

Renewing Your Mind

Most adults currently think in ways that stop them from reaching out to young people. If your church is to reach and keep young people effectively, its members must let their minds be renewed to more closely reflect the mind of Christ.

Ultimately, that renewal process is the work of God's Spirit in us, but Scripture encourages us to be yielded and active in the process (Romans 12:1-2, Philippians 2:5). Bible study, teaching, prayer, and (hopefully) books like this one can help speed that renewal of our minds.

In 1 Corinthians 2, Paul asks a question that Isaiah asked centuries earlier:

"Who has understood the mind of the LORD, or instructed Him as His counselor?"

Isaiah let it stand as a rhetorical question, implying that no one has understood the mind of the Lord—but Paul answers it. He adds, ***"But we have the mind of Christ."***

Admittedly, Paul says in the same letter, *Now we see but a poor reflection as in a mirror; then we shall see face to face,* (1 Corinthians 13:12), so, I assure you, I do not fully know the mind of Christ at this point in my life, but neither should we minimize the statement that we do know in part, because, Paul also wrote, *We have not received the spirit of the world, but the Spirit who is from God, that **we may understand what God has freely given us** (1 Corinthians 2:12),* so we are not able to dismiss it by saying, "Oh, well, he's just talking about some attitude here." No, call me a mystic, if you will, but we who are believers have understanding connected somehow to the mind and Spirit of Christ. If you soak in it for a while, it begins to have some amazing implications for us.

The Mind of Christ

According to Paul, we are able to know the mind of God today to a degree that even Isaiah could not. Our minds are not fully renewed, but no matter our theology, no matter our denomination, our minds are being renewed to reflect more and more the mind of Christ.

God is not hiding from us. He reveals Himself to us in His Word and by His Spirit. He wants to renew our minds, but if the Spirit of God lives in us, we have access to it to a degree that we may not fully understand, both in Scripture and in our spirits.

If we have the Spirit of God dwelling in us and have access to the mind of Christ, we are not normal folks. And we are free to be in a renewal process, rather than fearful someone will discover that we are not yet like Jesus.

7

God's Artistry

To more fully know the mind of Christ, we must look at Scripture, perhaps in a new way. From what I see in the Bible, God designed us to use pictures in our thinking, and He uses pictures to communicate truth to us. Almost every page of Scripture demonstrates God's willingness to use pictures to reveal His nature and His Truth. He uses pictures in four obvious arenas: Creation, His language, His ordinances, and the lives of His people. Let's look at each of the four briefly, in order to establish a biblical case for God's use of pictures to communicate to us.

Creation

Romans 1:20 demonstrates God's desire to reveal Himself to us in visual ways through Creation.

*"For since the creation of the world God's **invisible** qualities—His eternal power and divine nature—have been **clearly seen**, being understood from what has been made, so that men are without excuse."*

In Creation God spoke, and it was there to see. The invisible contents of His character are made visible in

Creation, and He made it beautiful. At the end of each day, He *"saw that it was good."*

We tend to think of God as this really intellectual, technical Clockmaker concerned about correctness and order, but He's also concerned about beauty and symmetry, like an Artist.

Notice that the first time in the Bible that God's Spirit came on a man, it gifted him in art. In Exodus 31:1-5, as the tabernacle is being prepared, we see the first example of someone filled with the Spirit of God and the result is art.

> *Then the LORD said to Moses, "See, I have chosen Bezalel . . . and **I have filled him with the Spirit of God**, with skill, ability and knowledge in all kinds of crafts—to make artistic designs for work in gold, silver and bronze, to cut and set stones, to work in wood, and to engage in all kinds of craftsmanship. . ."*

The pictures in the great Artist's visual mind were spoken into existence in Creation, and the pictures of His mind were put into creative artists by His Spirit.

Pictures in God's Language

God also uses pictures in His language. When God speaks directly to men, He uses word-pictures to make things clear to us.

God speaks in pictures, both when He Himself speaks and when He inspires the prophets to speak, or psalmists to write lyrics, or wise people to create proverbs. His word-pictures make spiritual concepts clearer for us. For instance, God described the nation of Israel to Jeremiah in pictures—an olive tree (Jeremiah 11:16), sheep (Jeremiah 23:2-3), and a daughter (Jeremiah 31:22).

One of the most famous word-pictures is, *The Lord is my shepherd.*" In Psalm 23, David uses a picture to compare God to a shepherd. Imagine how complicated it would be to explain the concept of God's relationship to us: His guarding, His caring, His leading, His discipline, His vigilance, and His authority, and our position as the defenseless followers trusting Him to take us through life in a way that is good for us. All of that is packaged in a simple picture: *'The Lord is my shepherd."*

The early singers of this Psalm understood shepherds. Through that picture they understood the Lord a little better and very quickly. Those word-pictures are called 'metaphors' by folks who study languages. They make abstract things concrete.

Notice how God uses a metaphor to explain the abstract concept of sin when He calls sin uncleanness. It's a metaphor that makes the abstract concept of sin into dirt or filth. It gets on us and sticks to us. It's not merely some behavior we did a while back; it gets in us and on us and stays. It needs attention. But there is a solution to our uncleanness—washing. David wrote in Psalm 51, *Wash me and I will be whiter than snow.*

Notice the layers of metaphor/comparison in that verse: Washing = forgiveness; white = spiritual purity, the result of washing/forgiveness; and the whiteness of our purity = that of snow.

Pictures in Ordinances

The ceremonies that God ordained (His ordinances) are also pictures that He provides to make the abstract clear for us. Consider the scapegoat in Leviticus 16. The high priest puts his hand on the head of the scapegoat and all the sin of the people is transferred to the goat, which then leaves the camp, taking all the sin with it. After that, the people know that their sins are gone! They didn't doubt their forgiveness. They saw their sin walk away on the goat.

God's pictures in ordinances connect to others with wonderful symmetry. Imagine the same scene of the scapegoat and the High Priest, but consider what it would be like if that High Priest refused to put his hand on the animal to transfer the sin? What if he left the sin on himself?

At first it would seem foolish, but that's what Jesus did! He is our High Priest. (Hebrews 6:20) In that role, He took on the sin of the people, but rather than transferring it, He kept it and became our Scapegoat! His willingness to humble Himself from High Priest to Scapegoat is part of what makes grace so amazing and so complete! As we'll see later, it also creates a picture of humility and sacrifice for us to imitate. God persistently uses these pictures in ceremonies to make abstract, spiritual things clear to us. He does it with other ordinances as well:

- *Circumcision*—the mark of God's covenant, now on our hearts
- *Baptism*—the death and rebirth into a new spiritual life
- *Marriage*—the picture of Jesus' love for the Church and a prophetic vision of their future reunion.
- *Communion*—the taking of Christ's body and blood into our bodies, uniting us with Him and us to one another.

They're concrete pictures that enable us to see an abstract truth in a physical action. They each remind us in physical ways of spiritual truth behind our identity and our relationship to God.

God's Pictures in People's Lives

God also gives us pictures through people's lives. For instance, Moses, Jonah, Noah, Joseph, and Hosea. God told Hosea to marry an adulterous woman. A tough assignment to live out, but a powerful visual aid to an entire nation to remind them that God's faithfulness is stronger than their unfaithfulness. God used Hosea's whole life as a parable for the people to illustrate His faithfulness and their unfaithfulness in Gomer.

Joseph is a more complex example. On one level, his life encourages us that, if we press through the trials we face, God is faithful and will use even the bad stuff to build His character and endurance in us. We may identify with Joseph in our suffering, but Joseph is also a picture of Jesus. In that light, we may more closely identify with Joseph's brothers in the story. Their sin sent Joseph into the pit, into slavery, false accusation, and imprisonment, as ours sent Jesus into the same. But Joseph was raised up to sit at the right-hand of the king, like Jesus, and those brothers, like us, deserved death for their sins against him. Then Joseph says words that Jesus could say, *"God sent me here to save you."* (Genesis 45)

It's a foreshadowing of grace, so the question is not, "Am I Joseph or is Jesus Joseph?" because Joseph was Joseph. He was a real man who lived a real life, but God used Joseph's life to paint a picture of the future Messiah and sculpt a model of faithfulness to encourage us. He also used the circumstances of Joseph's life to move His people into Egypt. This built the foundation for Moses' life to become a picture of God's power to deliver us from bondage, which foreshadows Christ's role as Deliverer. Through human lives we get hints or reflections of Jesus. In Jesus we get pictures that resonate back through all of history.

The Pictures Jesus Gave Us

Jesus was the Master of offering new pictures to reorganize His followers' thinking. In His parables, in His miracles, in His speech, in His life, in His death, and in His Resurrection, He offered pictures of God's Truth to His disciples. They had carried pictures in their minds from their Jewish or Greek cultures. Jesus replaced those old pictures with new ones again and again.

Another example: God's changing picture of the Temple! First, in the Old Testament, it's a tent, then a building. Then Jesus equates Himself with the Temple, saying He could rebuild it in three days if they destroyed it (John 2:19), which confused them until His Resurrection. But now each believer in Christ is a temple or a living stone in the temple. (1 Corinthians 6:19)

Another example: In the Temple the Jews sacrificed animals to God, but then Jesus is the sacrifice, the new Passover Lamb, but there's an even newer picture of sacrifice. In Romans 12, Paul says we are to be *"living sacrifices."* So our lives, like Joseph's life and the Passover Lamb, are to reflect a picture of Jesus to the world.

That's important. So let's summarize a bit:

Young people are leaving the church in astounding numbers. They may feel unwanted, untrusted, or lied to. To reach them well, we must have our minds renewed to more fully reflect the mind of Christ. We are designed to think in pictures, to use concrete images to organize our thinking and explanations of abstract concepts. God uses concrete pictures to reveal spiritual truth to His people. If we are in Christ, our minds are being made new. That means our minds' pictures are being redrawn. If our minds' pictures more closely reflect the mind of Christ, then our thinking, and eventually our behavior, will more accurately reflect the life of Jesus.

If much of Jesus' teaching was designed to repaint the pictures we think with, then it follows that we should prayerfully attempt to have our minds' pictures reflect those in the mind of Christ, so that in our thinking, our speech, and our lives, we will create pictures that God can use to demonstrate His truth to people.

In the remainder of this book, we'll look at a series of pictures or metaphors that many adults in the Church currently use to organize their thinking. For each concept, I'll suggest a new picture that may more closely approach the mind of Christ. We'll start with the picture we use to think and talk about concepts around the Gospel, and we'll build from there.

Part Three:
The Gospel

8

A Soil Problem?

In the parable of the sower, Jesus compared the spreading of the Gospel to the broadcasting of seeds. The seeds that fell on the rocky ground sprang up, but quickly withered. Is that what's going on with our young people? Do eighty percent of young people have a soil problem?

If a young person leaves our church, it may be an individual soil problem, but when so many are leaving, part of the problem may lie in the seed, our sowing method, or our care of young plants. In this section, we'll spend several chapters looking at the seed and the way we sow it. We'll review a common picture of the Gospel that many of us use to organize our thinking, our speech, and our behavior regarding salvation and Christian life. Then we'll discuss some potential implications on our attitudes and behaviors. Later, I'll offer a fresh picture that I pray will approach more closely the mind of Christ regarding salvation.

9

Separating Metaphors from Truth

I love my wife! She's lovely, and she's a treasure in my life. In almost 30 years together, the two of us have had three area codes, three children, three miscarriages, and three cancer surgeries. She still smiles at me and laughs at my jokes. She's a treasure! I'll say it again: I love her!

Now imagine I took a photograph of her. It is an adequate depiction, but not particularly flattering. I might put it in my wallet. It would be a nice reminder of her, but I might not show it off much. Sure, if people ask, I'll show it to them, but I'd likely apologize for its quality and explain that she's really much more lovely than this picture.

Contrast that to my behavior if a friend gave me a better picture of her, a lovely, candid photograph that captures her essence wonderfully well. Would I replace the old picture? Certainly!

I can change my pictures of my wife without offending her. She is unaffected by my picture changes, but my interactions with other people are profoundly affected by the picture change. The new one makes me want to talk about her and my marriage. It makes me bolder, more animated. I'd be eager to show the picture to people, knowing they would inevitably look at me and then look at her loveliness, and then back at me, and say, "Wow! How in the world did that happen?"

I'd take their question as an invitation to tell the story of the first time I saw her, and how I dated her long before she dated me, and how I tackled her in a mud puddle, and how blessed I am that she loved me even after all I've put her through. With my new picture, I would not apologize or be ashamed. I'd be eager to show everyone and tell them about my love for her.

In the same way that a renewed picture of my wife can affect my behavior, a renewed picture of the Gospel in my mind will change my behavior when I talk about Jesus, salvation, and the Christian life. But I say all of this to assure you that I am not talking about changing my wife or the Gospel, just the picture we have of each.

10

Our Current Picture: Jesus as the Life Bridge

The content of our Gospel presentation is typically communicated in various pictures. We draw on napkins or use printed materials with pictures of circles, trains, or thrones, but the most common picture is drawn something like this:

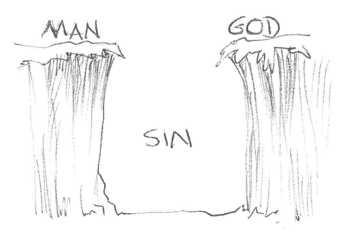

In this familiar picture, a man stands separated from God by a chasm of sin. His position is futile. His efforts to jump across in his own strength or build a bridge of good deeds will not be enough to get across the chasm. But Jesus became a Bridge to a new life. In His death on the cross, He spanned the chasm of sin to make a way for us to be in relationship with God the Father. Jesus became our Life Bridge.

Components of the Life-Bridge Picture

Let me be clear—I want to change this picture. In the next few chapters, we'll look at the individual components of the old picture, including the sinner and his side of the chasm, Jesus, the chasm of sin, God, and the movement involved in salvation.

The Sinner

The Sinner is fine.

By all appearances, our sinner on the left cliff is doing okay. He is pondering his situation and the opportunity before him, but there is no immediate threat to the sinner in the picture. Certainly if he dies, the consequences are grave (pardon the pun), but if our sinner is young, death most probably seems a distant event, giving him little motivation to choose quickly. He might reason that if the Cross is there for him now, then it will be there for him when he is older. He need not make the decision now.

From this picture he has not dived into sin; sin is simply a barrier to his relationship with God. The sinner could reason, "Sure, I am separated from God, but I am on an equal plane with Him. And I can still see God from here . . . He's just over there! If I get in a jam, then I'll just move across the Life-Bridge. What's the problem with where I am right now?"

The Christian is fine; he's with God.

With this picture in mind, the sinner has little urgency to make a choice, therefore we have little urgency as potential evangelists to interrupt his life with the Gospel. Why would we? We have crossed the chasm to join God's side. We are safe and sound, so we are fine too.

Our friend the sinner may be sad or troubled, but we often lack the motivation to leave our comfortable spot and intrude on his apparently painless situation. Some of us may wait for God's promptings in our lives before we talk to him. Some may trust that he'll cross when God predestines it, and others will hope that he will choose wisely. Until then, we will all pray for him, or simply ignore him, though some may leave him a tract. But this picture gives us little direction and little motivation to offer the Good News of salvation with boldness and confidence.

Movement toward sin to reach God.

In the Life-Bridge picture, the sinner must venture **toward** the chasm of sin to reach God. Does moving someone closer to sin take him on the path toward God? It feels contrary to the concept of "repentance," a word-picture of turning away from sin.

With this current picture organizing their thinking, some unbelievers could reason that a simple move to the left, away from God, also moves them away from the danger of falling into sin or feeling the pain of separation. A stroll to the left might seem a wiser move for the immediate future, allowing them to avoid sin, the risk of an untested bridge, and the guilt of not responding to the calls of those on the other side.

11

Crossing the Life Bridge

Christendom as Unfamiliar Territory

To the sinner standing on the left cliff, the other side may seem a mysterious land where Christians go to die. Crossing the bridge requires the sinner to cross to an unfamiliar space occupied by an unfamiliar God. Such a move may feel riskier than standing still.

Potential for Pride

Our current picture of the Life Bridge may contribute to a Christian's tendency to feel wiser and more deserving than the sinners. Those of us who crossed the Life Bridge may believe we made the good and wise choice, thus our unsaved friend seems foolish for refusing God's generosity. If I think him a fool, my prayer may sound something like this: "Thank you, God, that I am not like that foolish sinner," which echoes the prayer of the Pharisee that Jesus rebuked in this parable found in Luke 18:10-14.

> *Two men went up to the temple to pray, one a Pharisee and the other a tax collector. The Pharisee stood up and prayed about himself: "God, I thank You that I am not like other men—*

robbers, evildoers, adulterers—or even like this tax collector." But the tax collector stood at a distance. He would not even look up to heaven, but beat his breast and said, "God, have mercy on me, a sinner."

I tell you that this man, rather than the other, went home justified before God. For everyone who exalts himself will be humbled, and he who humbles himself will be exalted.

Any attitude that causes us to look down on the lost does not reflect the mind of Christ.

Movement Away from Sinners at Salvation

If we embrace this Life-Bridge picture, our movement at salvation requires that we leave our unsaved friends behind. Our move to a different place with a different people makes it difficult to justify remaining in relationship with those outside the Church.

Avoiding the Pain the Sinner Causes

Some believers are wonderfully compassionate and merciful individuals. For them, the delay in the salvation of the lost person becomes a source of disappointment, grief, or pain: "Come to Jesus! It hurts me to see you refusing. I don't like feeling this pain and disappointment when you reject God's offer. I need you to ease the pain."

In response, merciful Christians may simply increasingly avoid the sinner to avoid the grief they face in the relationship. Over time, they have few friends outside the Church.

Fearing

In the Life-Bridge picture, if we see the Church (Greek *ecclesia*, "those called out,") as "those called out from among the sinners," we create distance from sinners, and we may grow fearful of them. That fear may drive us into what some call a "holy huddle" or a Christian "bubble." In this scenario, all my friends share my faith, my age (as we will see later), and my values. I develop a strong sense of "us" vs. "them."

Booing

When a church embraces this picture of the sinners as being on the "other side," it eventually builds defenses against them. We're supposed to be sharing the "Gospel" here, a word that means "Good News," but I've been with congregations that booed particular politicians. They've booed homosexuals. They've booed the New York Times! Who are we to boo anyone? When did we become the mob crying, "Crucify!"?

With the Life-Bridge picture organizing our thinking, we may see unbelievers as fools for their failure to cross. We may even accuse them, saying, "They are ruining our country and our culture. I must fight them. We must take back the nation from them!"

With that heated attitude behind it, the collective voice of the Church may sound angry, resentful, or arrogant to those outside. When we speak to them as the enemy, they hear their enemy's voice and may become more resistant to the message of Christ.

Also, when the Church speaks to the outsider as the enemy, she damages the reputation of Christ. When the Church speaks from a position of power, trying to rule from above, it runs contrary to the Spirit of Christ, who came as a servant. Yes, Jesus sometimes spoke harshly, but only to those who believed they were above the rest or knew better than others. Jesus reserved His anger for the religious people. He didn't high-five the disciple who cut off an ear of His accusers—He healed the wound.

The inappropriate tone in our collective voice has tended to create resistance against the Church, which we call "persecution" and "suffering," rather than seeing it as a reasonable response by people to our arrogant tone. Further, it blurs our message of the Father's love. Yes, we can call sin, sin, but grief may better reflect the mind of Christ toward the lost.

Rather than playing the victim of persecution, perhaps we should apologize, or at least ask if an apology is necessary, and guard our hearts in the future from an attitude toward sinners that is not reflective of the mind of Christ.

Yet, if we respond to sinners with anger, we ignore the command of Jesus to love our enemies, or Paul's admonition that we *"battle not against flesh and blood."* The Gospel presented well will smell like death to some (2 Corinthians 2:16), and some will react to your most Christ-like love with venom. Persecution will come; people will hate us, but our hearts and minds must be reflective of the mind of Christ, who was willing to lay down His life for us while we were still sinners, and who asks us to do the same for the sinners around us.

Christ's Bride is most gorgeous, most attractive when her intent is to delight in Him and to reflect His love to those around her with humility and service. When all they hear from her is scolding and correcting, she is not lovely, and those she scolds will mock her as a nag.

12

The Divine in the Life-Bridge Picture

The Father Unmoved

Notice that in the Life-Bridge picture, God never moves. He is stationed there in heaven, apparently undisturbed, distant from the sinner's plight. He offers salvation by sending Jesus. Jesus allows us access to God, but this apparent passivity of God undermines our talk of a "personal relationship" with God or the intimate love of the Father for us. In this picture, He keeps His distance until we move to Him.

A Wooden Jesus

Our picture of the Gospel must accurately portray the identity and role of Jesus, yet the Life-Bridge fails in several ways. First, Jesus is represented by a wooden cross, not a Person who felt pain. How do we have a personal relationship with wood?

Second, for we who have crossed the Life Bridge, Jesus is now behind us. He has served His purpose or is still serving His purpose as a Bridge for sinners. Third, Jesus appears passive, a messenger and sacrifice sent at the Father's command. We may tend to demote Him to an obedient instrument used to accomplish the Father's will. As we will discuss, He is much more than that.

Conclusions

My intent overall is to aid the renewal of your mind to more fully reflect the mind of Christ, and subsequently help you and your church develop young people into lifelong disciples of Jesus. The picture we use to organize our thinking and communication of the Gospel is key in that renewal.

Certainly the organizing picture of Jesus as Life Bridge is simple and effective in producing initial salvations; however, it may have contributed to some problems in the collective heart of the Church. Filtered through this picture, our evangelism may be less than energetic and offer a less-than-glorious picture of the Living Water for which the world thirsts.

As in the pictures of my wife, the Life-Bridge picture is that merely adequate picture. It communicates the components of the message, yet the picture needs renewing, because it—

- is not a biblical picture
- does not represent the Person, movement, or attitude of Christ effectively
- does not represent the sinner correctly
- may dampen our enthusiasm about evangelism, and
- may contribute to attitudes in us that are less than loving.

In short, we need a new picture that will help us experience the same boldness, clarity, urgency, and humility that we see in Peter, Paul, and early evangelists in Scripture. It should move us toward the lost, not distance us from them, and it should call us to the imitation of Christ, not to the imitation of the world. Our picture should also reflect the Gospel as the Good News and bring great joy to our lives and to those who hear it. We need a new picture.

13

A New Picture of the Gospel

Our New Picture of the Gospel

Repainting the pictures we use to conceptualize the Gospel to a more biblical image will increase our effectiveness as evangelists. We will include most of the same components used in the previous picture (Sinner, Sin, God, Jesus, etc.), but their nature and their movements will change significantly. We'll take them in the same order as earlier.

The Sinner

When we left our sinner, he was standing on the left side of a chasm of sin, considering the move toward God across the Life Bridge of Jesus.

That position, his posture, and his state are not biblically accurate. With three words in one verse, Paul hurls our sinner into a more difficult place: *"As for you, you were **dead in your** transgressions and sins..."* *(Ephesians 2:1)*

It's not looking good for our sinner. He's not fine.

In Sin

First, Paul says we are **IN** sin. Therefore we are NOT standing safely across from God separated from him by a chasm. There is no left side! There is no safe holding area where we can consider our options apart from sin. Moving to the left away from sin is not an option. Without Christ, we are in the chasm!

Dead in Sin

Further, before salvation, we were not merely "in sin," we were "dead in sin." It is a spiritual death passed to us through the generations from Adam. We are born dead in our sin.

It is not a new picture for Paul. He'd read of it in Numbers 12:11-12. Moses' sister Miriam is struck with a skin disease. Aaron pleads with Moses using this same picture of a birth into death to describe the results of her sin, and perhaps describing ours: *"Please, my lord, do not hold against us the sin we have so foolishly committed. Do not let her be like a stillborn infant coming from its mother's womb with its flesh half eaten away."*

Apart from Christ, we are stillborn. So our new picture of the sinner is revised to look like this:

We need to be born again (one of those wonderful pictures that Jesus used to renew the minds of His disciples and Nicodemus).

Dead in YOUR Sin

Paul makes it clear that sin is not a distant conceptual barrier between God and us. That sin was ours before we met Christ. It had our name on it. It wasn't outside us, not a hindrance *between* God and us; it was *our* hindrance and we were *in* it. If it was merely a concept outside us, unattached to anyone, God could have dealt with it differently. But because we owned it, the guilt for it and the debt required as a result of it were our responsibility.

But it's a bit more complicated than "I own my sin." The Bible says before we come to Christ, we are *"slaves to sin." (John 8:34)* That complicates our picture of ownership. To illustrate, I'll use God's word-picture from Genesis 4: sin as a hungry lion, waiting for opportunity to pounce on Cain. *"Sin is **crouching** at your door; it desires to have you..."*

My Lion

With that in mind, imagine that before I was in Christ I inherited a lion; he's been in the family for generations. I have the papers to prove it! My address is on his collar. I am his owner! I feed and care for him. Legally, he is my lion!

He eats a great deal, including neighbors and family members. When he does eat someone, I'm ashamed. His behavior reflects badly on me as his owner, since everyone knows he's MY lion, including the judge, who's made it clear that it's against the law to own lions where I live, and illegal to let them eat people. The judge has declared that I must pay for the damages my lion has caused and the lives my lion ate. But I can't seem to get rid of this troublesome lion. I had hoped to master him one day. I'd be so proud—the envy of my neighborhood (at least what's left of it).

But I've discovered that the chain that leads from his collar is attached to *my* collar. I own him, but he is my master.

At some point, I realized my lion had consumed me. I was IN him. And I was dead in him. So, without Christ, I lie spiritually dead in the belly of a lion that I own. I need help.

So, like that lion, that sin was MY sin; I was responsible for the payments required on it. It was something I was required to handle. On the other hand, sin owned me. It was MY master; I was the slave. I was chained to it, obligated to it, and I am unable to be free myself. Further, I was dead inside my sin, unable to see truth, unable to hear the cries of my friends who have been set free until I was first resurrected by some miraculous power.

All orthodox streams of Christianity flow past the common ground that lost folks are in need of a Savior. Our unbelieving friends are in a difficult predicament, not simply separated from God, but in a position that requires significant intervention. They need more than a safe crossing point and wisdom to make a good choice. They need:

A Hero to come to them,

Resurrection or Rebirth,

Release from the chains of sin,

Extraction from within their sin,

Freedom from the debt of their sin, and,

as our former picture portrayed, a restored relationship with God.

Implications

At this point, consider this: how do we best respond to those who are dead and enslaved in their sins?

Compassion

First, our friend the sinner is to be pitied or mourned, not attacked for his foolishness or his damage to the culture. He's not the enemy! He's a casualty or a prisoner in the enemy's war against Man. He may be a victim of deception and appear to be a traitor in that war. He may persecute Christians, but Paul understood *"our struggle is not against flesh and blood" (Ephesians 6:2)* because, before his encounter with Christ, Paul was persecuting the Church and seemed an unlikely candidate for salvation (yet the most unlikely convert became one of the most powerful). Rather than demonize the unbeliever, we'd do well to pray for his salvation.

Patience

By shifting the sinner in our picture into the pit of sin and subsequently shifting our attitude, perhaps we can experience a new patience for those who continue in their sin before they believe. What else would we expect from them until they know Jesus and freedom from their slavery?

Also, a sinner's lack of response to your Gospel presentation is the normal and reasonable response of a swallowed corpse when confronted with the truth. Logic is not enough to release him. Knowledge is not enough. Even the Truth is not enough to resurrect him. His extraction from sin will first require the Spirit of God to act in grace.

Similarly, Lazarus did not make the wise choice in being brought back to life. Nor can he boast of having faith to come out of the tomb. How much faith did Lazarus have when he was dead? He was dead. Life came to him, and he heard the message in the word of Christ to come out. Then faith came, just as we see in Romans 10:17, *"Faith comes from hearing the message, and the message is heard through the word of Christ."*

Before salvation, the sinner's state is not hopeless. As we will see in the next component, we are not free to turn away from the sinner in despair. With Lazarus in mind, we can see the Church (ecclesia = called out) as those called out of sin and death, not called to huddle away from sinners for fear that they may pollute us.

With this new picture of the sinner, we may experience a new urgency to pray for him, to beg God for mercy on his behalf, and to move toward him in powerful ways.

14

The Divine Components of Our Gospel Picture

While the shift in perception of the sinner is significant, the biggest shift in our new picture is the identity and role of Jesus.

Emmanuel—God with us

We sing about Emmanuel at Christmas, but consider the picture of Jesus as portrayed in Philippians 2:5-8:

> *Your attitude* (Greek=*Phreneo* "mind")
> *should be the same as that of Christ Jesus:*
> *Who, being in very nature God,*
> *did not consider equality with God*
> *something to be grasped,*
> *but made Himself nothing,*
> *taking the very nature of a servant,*
> *being made in human likeness.*
> *And being found in appearance as a man,*
> *He humbled Himself*
> *and became obedient to death—*
> *even death on a cross!*

Our previous picture of Jesus as the Life Bridge communicated the generosity of God in making a way for us through Christ. This picture in Philippians emphasizes the "Godness" of Christ and His willingness to empty Himself to take on human form and face death to bring life to us. This passage portrays Jesus as God, not a subservient heavenly messenger forced by the Father to go toward us, not an obedient vessel to carry His message. He was God who came to us.

This also disrupts the Life-Bridge portrayal of God as the passive and distant King, waiting for us comfortably on His throne while His messenger Jesus does His dirty work.

This new picture promotes Christ to equality with the Father and helps us begin to fathom the Father's Agape love, that He would sacrifice so much for us, and better illustrates the Son's example of laying down more than His human life. Let's unpack a few components.

God to Us

In addition to this humbling identity change, our new picture portrays His movement differently. He did not come to be a passive bridge safely spanning the chasm of sin. He did not come merely *toward* us, so we could go toward Him; He came all the way *to* us. He dove into the world like a lifeguard at a sewage plant, enduring unimaginable filth and pain to rescue us and resuscitate us, sacrificing His life for ours.

One implication of this movement to us is clear: Our current discipleship and worship methods focus on our need to move toward God. Whether it be in Bible study, singing, prayer, meditation, or whatever behavior seems to "work," we look for something to make us feel some satisfaction at moving closer to God.

Consider this illustration: When my friend Janeene got married outside a friend's home on a lovely evening in July, Cory her groom walked from behind the house and stood at the base of the front porch steps waiting for his bride to arrive. It was just as they had rehearsed, but Janeene had a surprise for Cory. When it was time for her to enter and come down the aisle, Janeene began to sing *"Fly"* by Nicole Nordeman, a lovely song, and Janeene has an amazing voice. It was a glorious moment.

I realized that Janeene's movement toward Cory was a picture of true worship. Her worship was not the song or the singing; it was her, offering her whole self to him, moving toward him to be one with him. That made it even more beautiful!

Janeene's movement toward Cory felt big and dramatic, until I remembered that Cory came all the way across the country, leaving behind his security, his family, and home, to be with his bride.

Likewise, if the groom is a picture of Jesus, then our attempts to move toward God and please Him with our obedience, our songs, and surrender feel big and significant. When we do it right, it feels like growth or progress. But what if we reframe the picture to help us understand that God (like Cory) left the security and ease of heaven and moved toward us in Christ Jesus. Therefore, His move toward us dwarfs any move we make toward Him. Therefore, our only reasonable response is worship, not just singing, but offering our whole selves to Him as living sacrifices. Any effort we make to be righteous and please Him is like filthy rags compared to the righteousness we have been given by Christ. That should put the amazing back in your grace!

The Emptying of Christ

Further, if Jesus did not simply give up His life for us, but gave up the glory, ease, and safety of heaven, then the big loss for Jesus is not death on a cross; the big loss is giving up heaven, giving up equality with God and the form of God to become a baby, then a man, and then a corpse. He who created everything made Himself nothing. His love for us pressed Him out of the comfort of heaven to come into our pit of sin and pain, to take our death and give us His life.

The Work of Christ

Jesus did more than make a way for us. Jesus took on our death and our chains. Consequently, we gain life and freedom. In other words, He crawled into the belly of our lion to take our place and give us His place in life, free from the debt, the penalty, and the guilt of our sin. But, as you know, Jesus did not remain in the lion. The Bible says,

"The Spirit of the LORD came upon him in power, so that he tore the lion apart with his bare hands as he might have torn a young goat."

That picture from Judges 14:6 of Samson's defeat of the lion resonates with our picture of Christ's resurrection. It foreshadows the Messiah's defeat of sin. Some time later, Samson returns to the lion and finds honey there, which he shares with others. Later, in verse 14, he tells a riddle:

"Out of the eater, something to eat;
out of the strong, something sweet."

For three days, the people could not answer his riddle. It was impossible to understand until they had the proper picture in mind. Without that picture, the riddle made no sense and seemed frustratingly foolish, but with the picture of the lion and the honey in your mind, the answer is clear. Pictures make things clear, even for Philistines.

But God's pictures come in layers. Samson's riddle has connections to Christ (the sweetness that came from out of the tomb), and to Communion (that which we eat and share). In our sharing of it, we become the sweetness that Christ pulled out of our death (our enemy) after He defeated it. Our message is that sweetness is to be shared with those around us in the world. I suppose we were the Philistines at some point, unable to see what was so obvious until we had the right picture in our heads.

In still another layer, we become the ones who imitate Samson as Christ to find those who are now in the defeated lion but are destined to be the sweetness of Christ.

Christ as the Stranger

Our picture of Jesus leaving the ease of heaven and arriving as the stranger who joins a tribe, loves the tribe, and sacrifices Himself to rescue the tribe is not a "new" picture of the Gospel at all; it's the old picture. It has worked throughout Church history. Paul reflected it when in his travels he became "all things to all people," even the Gentiles, and offered his life for the sake of the Gospel.

In 432 A.D., Patrick (later St. Patrick) left the ease and glory of Rome and arrived as a missionary in what is now Ireland, but then was a land of wandering tribes. He showed up in their world at age 48 as a stranger, and spent his life serving them. He lived among the people, prayed for them, and lived his life as a follower of Jesus.[3] 48 years later, he died, leaving behind a nation transformed, a culture of hunter-gatherers now living in communities, each with a church built at its center, because one man, and then his disciples, and then their disciples gave those wandering tribes a clear picture of Jesus in their words and their lives.

There's something in us that resonates with the picture of the stranger who arrives as a mysterious outsider, who joins the tribe, loves the tribe, and gives his life to rescue the tribe. It is the story of Moses. It is the story of Joseph, and it is the story of Jesus. More curiously, it is the plot of movies like *Shane, Dances with Wolves,* Disney's *Pocahontas, The Last Samurai, The Book of Eli, Terminator: The Last Salvation, Avatar,* and others.

And it is our story. We are designed and equipped by God as new creations in Christ to live it out—to be the

---

[3] (See George G. Hunter's fine book on this topic: *Celtic Evangelism,* Abingdon Press, 2000.)

stranger in a strange land who joins the tribe, loves, and sacrifices for them. The rest of the world hopes for it and knows it when they see it. If we gain a renewed picture of the Gospel and our minds are renewed, then we'll live differently, and the young people around us will see in our lives a vague but life-giving reflection of Jesus.

Summary

God was not passive; He came after us.

He was not distant and safe; He was with us and suffered for us.

He was not seated comfortably on a distant throne; He hung naked on a cross.

He didn't send us a hero to rescue us; He became the Hero and rescued us Himself.

When we really begin to understand what "God with us" means, the only reasonable response to our new picture of the Gospel is worship and awe.

15

Implications for Our Movement

The contrast between the Life-Bridge picture and this revised picture of Jesus in Philippians 2 is clear, but clearer still are the instructions that come in that passage: ***"Let your attitude (mind) be like that of Christ Jesus . . ."***

We are to think like Christ. We are to imitate Christ, first in our hearts and then in our actions. We are to demonstrate the same movement, the same humility, the same emptying. **This is the key to reaching young people effectively.** If we don't move toward them in love and humility, young people won't respond well to the Gospel. But they don't want adults to simply move toward them; they want us to move toward them imitating Christ as best we can in attitude and action. They don't need us to do it perfectly; they just need us to be willing to try and, God willing, to reflect Christ.

Churches around the world are trying to figure out how to reach young people. If we continue to think in terms of developing programs to bring in young people, our churches will die a slow death. We will reach them only to the degree that the individuals in our particular church are willing to—

> humble ourselves;
>
> empty ourselves;
>
> leave our safe places;
>
> show up in their lives;
>
> share the wisdom and life we have found in Christ;

and love them well.

It's quite a responsibility to imitate the movement of Christ. We'll fall horribly short of His example, but in our moving toward young people to both speak and demonstrate the love of Christ, they may see sketches of His love. If we try to share the Gospel in safe ways (such as leaving tracts), they may resent us. If we try to share the love of Christ from a safe distance, we confuse the picture of what Jesus has done for them and ignore what He did for us.

Specks and Logs

We're more like the Pharisees than we like to admit. Rather than dealing with their hearts, we want to deal with their specks. If we see young people behaving badly at church or in the neighborhood, we often want to be their schoolmaster, to correct them, to position ourselves above them, and speak down to them. The specks of immaturity in their eyes are so easy to identify! And so easy to address—a quick flick, and their speck is gone. But the mind of Christ would have us first look at the log in our eye.

The problem for me is that my log (and perhaps yours) feels like a permanent fixture in my life. I've carved and polished it over the years to become an ugly accessory to my personality. On my worst days, my log is large enough to hide behind. Some days it feels like it protects me, like an essential part of my wardrobe, without which I would feel exposed. My log has learned to talk, but it lies to me and says I must pursue comfort and avoid being disturbed. It tells me it's best that I deal with specks in kids' eyes. But it needs to go.

Philippians 2 reminds me of the real question: "What can **we** do today with our words, our actions, and our lives to give the young people around us a clearer picture of Jesus? How can my life reflect the movement of Christ?"

Our Movement toward Them

When we leave our safe places to move toward a young person in imitation of Christ, we get to be "incarnational," or Jesus "in the flesh" to them. In those encounters, they will get a glimpse of Jesus. Some people only get a few examples in a lifetime, but most Christians can remember a time when an adult believer persistently moved toward them when they were young and demonstrated the love of Christ in a way that was important for their faith development.

Hal Uzzel was a man who reflected Christ to me again and again as I grew up; I'll never forget the first time. I was about 16 years old, and I was walking back to my seat in the balcony during a teaching weekend offered by my church. I was a little late, and the guest preacher had already begun. As I approached my seat, Hal got up from his seat and came quickly to me. He looked very serious. I thought I was in trouble, but he grabbed me above my elbow and turned me toward the front of the church. He pointed at the guest preacher, then he leaned in close and whispered, "One day that's going to be you up there."

Then he looked at me, smiled, patted me on the shoulder, and returned to his seat. At the time I thought, "Silly old man," but I never forgot it. There were other times when he spoke to me that way on various topics, but I think of that first moment every time I walk into a church to preach. Somehow God let Hal Uzzel see something in me, energized him to get out of his comfortable chair, and speak words to me that had life in them.

Pastor Percy Burns continues to reflect Jesus to me. Percy loved me well when I served as the youth pastor under his leadership. He gave me a new picture of Jesus and His loving authority.

Percy had authority over me, but he didn't use it to protect himself and his reputation. He persistently offered the truth in love. He always encouraged me, "Take more risks."

And when my risks went badly, he laughed and gave me a clear and wise path to walk forward. He addressed my mistakes with patience, and when I did something well, he celebrated with me. But I felt most loved when he would simply step out of his schedule and come down the hall to my office, sit on my office couch, and say, "Scott, Scott, Scott! How are things in your world?"

Just showing up and showing concern reflected the love of Christ to me. Percy also loved me well when he invited me (or forced me) to follow him into ministry situations that felt way over my head. I felt trusted, or at least saw his trust in God to work through me. Even today, Percy's life sketches out a precious picture of Jesus for me, one I try to carry with me into ministry and life.

Using their lives as ink, Hal and Percy drew pictures of Jesus for me. I have been blessed with lots of those pictures from too many individuals to list. None of them reflected Him perfectly, but in their collective, loving movement to me, and in their willingness to speak life and truth to me, they each pointed me toward Him.

Every healthy adult Christian I know can name those people in their lives—pastors, youth pastors, small group leaders, or just an interested adult. Encouraged by those kinds of examples, we now have the opportunity to do the same for young people around us who need it desperately, so it is appropriate to add two components to our Gospel picture that were missing in the first picture: First, the incarnational role of the Church in the spread of the Gospel.

So our picture is now this:

Jesus came to us . . .

. . . so we move toward the world in imitation of Christ

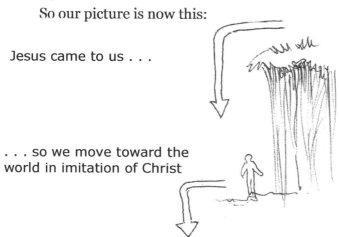

Our response to the movement of Christ toward us is not our movement toward God; it is our imitation of Christ, our movement toward the lost and the hurting. We go to them speaking the truth in love, not demanding that they respond but hoping and praying they do. And when they don't, rather than scolding them, we can grieve for them.

The second component required is the Holy Spirit. When we imitate Jesus we are not Jesus, but neither are we mere men. The Holy Spirit dwells in us, so we go out in power, empowered with the gifts and the fruit of the Spirit.

Conclusion

Revising our picture of the Gospel to more closely approach the mind of Christ decreases our fear and presses us joyfully out of our safe routines and into the lives of other people in the imitation and incarnation of Christ.

Still it is not merely our pictures of the Gospel that stop us from reaching out to young people. It is also our foundational perceptions of those young people that make us reluctant to move toward them. In the coming chapters, I will identify some common perceptions of young people and offer a replacement picture that will reduce our fear and embolden us to move toward them in Christ-like ways that will change their lives.

Part Four:
Young People

16

Current Pictures of Young People

Imagine you are about to go out your front door to get the mail from the box on the street, but through your front window you see a pack of young people roaming down your street. Their clothing is odd and perhaps inappropriate by your standards. They are all laughing, but you're not sure why. The pack stops, and one of the young studs with strange hair, the alpha male, starts drumming on your mailbox to impress the girls. Two of the younger girls start shaking their tails to the beat. An older boy barks at two skinny boys who then gallop onto your lawn. The older boy pursues them and pulls one down to the ground almost at your front steps.

How do you feel? Do you go out to get your mail? Or do you wait?

If you are like most adults, you may feel a little threatened. That's normal, but Christians are not called to be normal; we are to have the mind of Christ. If a church hopes to reach out to young people, its members must be willing to leave the safe places of our lives to move toward them. Our fear acts as a barrier to that movement.

In the first chapter of this section, we'll look at the pictures in our minds that may cause that fear. They are pictures that quietly undermine our efforts to reach and love young people well. We'll look at three of them. In them you will better understand why adults may feel afraid of young people, and in the subsequent chapters I'll offer new pictures that will reduce that fear so we can love well.

Picture One

Jesus said, *"From the overflow of our hearts, the mouth speaks."* (Luke 6:45) The way we talk reflects the condition of our heart. That's important to our mind's renewal, and it's important that by listening carefully to the speech of individuals, we can discern the pictures that they use to organize their thinking. With that in mind, consider the following scene, which includes a collection of common phrases adults use to talk about young people.

Two church deacons stand in the aisle of a sanctuary between services.

Bob: "Look at those **kids** out in the hall!"

Jerry: "It'd take a **cattle prod** to **corral** them into Sunday school."

Bob: "Yep, like **herdin' cats**...I think that youth pastor needs a **whip and a chair** to give 'em a little discipline, **tame** 'em down, or at least **rein** 'em in a bit."

Jerry: "Yep, but that children's pastor? She keeps her **rug-rats** and **curtain-climbers** in line."

Bob: "Suppose so, but those **ankle-biters** are easier to **tame** than these **monsters.** They're **wild**!"

Gladys, a formal, rather stuffy woman, approaches the two. "Oh, I dare say, the behavior of that Thomas boy is just **beastly**."

Bob: "Yes, ma'am, last week that **turkey** and a couple other **strays** broke in line at the picnic."

Bob: "They **swarmed** past me in a **stampede** and **pounced** on the fried chicken. And once they got their **paws** on the biscuits, it looked like a **feeding frenzy**, I tell ya! Once they **wolfed** down the biscuits, they **scurried** over to the desserts."

Jerry: "They were in the parking lot later, **monkeyin'** around with my RV. I told them to knock off the **horseplay,** and that Thomas boy had the nerve to snap back at me, 'Leave us alone, ya old **goat!**' Some nerve! That boy needs some **training**."

Gladys: "Those a**nimals!**"

Review the words in bold print. If speech is the overflow of the heart, what is the perception that steers the heart of these adults?

Clearly their speech suggests a picture of young people as animals.[4]

With the picture revealed, review the very first paragraph in this chapter. Notice the animal images I used. The group passing in front of your house was "a pack" of "kids" (baby goats) "roaming" the streets. They "shake their tails," "stalk," and "gallop." The language seems harmless enough, but in our minds, packs are feral, carnivorous, and instinctual, and therefore dangerous. We fear animals we don't know. Any wise person would

---

[4] Others are less harsh and equate young people with the uncivilized human. Typically their comments are offensive to young people and to tribal peoples. We say,

"They act like a bunch of savages!"

"They're like a bunch of barbarians."

"They're on the warpath again."

"The natives are restless."

stay indoors until a roaming pack of animals is gone. Also notice the offense that Jerry and his friends take in his being called an old "goat," while they use all types of animal imagery including "kids" (baby goats) to describe the young people.

It would be wonderful if kids would take the first step. For instance, if one would say, "Hello, I'm the troubled Thomas boy. I sense from your avoidance of me that you are scared of me. There is no need to be! I act angry at the world, because it makes me feel more powerful than just feeling scared all the time. I just wanted you to know that. Call me sometime; I need adults in my life. Have a great day."

But most don't have the maturity to do that. Most adults don't either, but neither do we need to be afraid of youths without cause. We are God's people. Our spiritual ancestors have a history of miraculous safety in the lion's den. If our mind's perception of young people as animals makes us afraid of them and less loving toward them, then we need to replace the picture.

In the mind of Christ, young people are not animals. As we saw earlier in the Gospel, Jesus moved toward young people, and He wants them to come to Him. To Him they are people with the same fears, needs, and hopes that we have, but with less experience and perhaps less wisdom.

Picture Two

Again from the overflow of our hearts, here are comments I've heard from Christian adults about young people:

"They don't know how to behave in public."

"I can't understand a word they're saying."

"The things they wear!"

"She's not wearing enough clothes to flag down a train!"

"I can't imagine why people would do that to their bodies."

"Turn down that racket. That's not music!"

"Is that real hair?"

Those comments are things we might say about people we see in a National Geographic magazine. They reveal a controlling metaphor that depicts young people as aliens from a foreign land or a different planet.

At a church where I spoke recently, one mother said to me, "I think when my daughter was 15, body-snatchers came from outer space and replaced her with someone else. Sometimes I ask myself, "Who is this girl and what have you done with my daughter?"

Those pictures of young people as foreigners or aliens are reinforced when the young people don't obey the unwritten rules of our culture (wearing hats indoors, shaking hands limply, talking at inappropriate times, or sporting tattoos formerly reserved for crusty sailors or outlaw motorcyclists). Since they don't know the rules, they seem to be part of a foreign culture. We are scared of foreigners. When we talk of them, we seem to underline the pronoun to set *them* in strong contrast to <u>us</u>. *We* don't trust *them*. When *they* laugh, *we* fear *they* are laughing at <u>us</u>. When *they* whisper, *we* suspect *they* are talking about <u>us</u>. As we discussed earlier, young people who feel treated like foreigners, who feel untrusted, will leave our churches.

If we see young people as foreigners, we do not have the mind of Christ, and we will not reach them as long as we view them as part of a separate culture. We need a new image to represent them. They are not foreigners to God.

Picture Three

The last picture in this section is evident when adults talk about their perceptions of relationships around young people. Groups of young people may be described as:

A *circle,* a *knot,* or *ring* of friends

A *huddle* or a *cluster*

A *band* or a *tribe*

Their own little club

Their friendships may be *very tight.*

They may not *let you in,* and you may feel *shut out* of their "clique" (French for "latch"). Those not part of the "in" crowd are <u>outcasts</u>, not *in* style, but *out* of style.

Parents struggling to connect with their children may ask them to *open up,* but are disappointed when they just *shut down* or *shut up.* Those kids may complain that adults or parents are "*in* the way," "*in* their space," "*in* their faces," or "*in* my business," and they say they want parents *out—out* of the way, *out* of my room, and *out* of my life.

This image is more sophisticated, but equally damaging to our ability to reach them.

All of this suggests that young people are closed spaces adults cannot enter. They are locked doors to which adults don't have keys. The closed-spaces image is built on another perception that portrays human relationships as spaces having a clear "in" and a clear "out." (I'm *in* a relationship, *in* love, *in*volved, or *en*tangled, vs. *out* of a relationship, *out* of love, available, or free.)

Being *out* when you want to be *in* feels bad. Trying to get in and being rejected feels worse, so we avoid it. The whole *in-vs.-out* and *us-vs.-them* imagery is rooted in fear and rejection—our fear of young people and their fear of us, and our desire to avoid rejection and their desire to do the same.

Honestly, some young people may not want you to have the key that opens them, and you have to be prayerful and wise about the timing and manner of your move toward them, especially if the young person has been wounded.

But this metaphor of young people as closed spaces is not reflective of the mind of Christ. He does not see them as closed and locked spaces. This picture is a lie we use to protect ourselves from rejection, a reason to avoid moving toward them so we can protect ourselves. Loving relationships are perhaps better seen as a journey, rather than a clear in or out status. We grow closer over time without the need to feel rejected if a scared young person reacts poorly to our efforts to love him well.

Whether we see young people as animals, foreigners, or a closed group, they may seem dangerous or unapproachable. We shrink back from young people, even our own kids, when we think with these pictures. We get into a cycle of "I avoid you, you avoid me" and round and round we go.

Simply yelling, "Be strong and courageous!" will not make adults respond differently to young people; it is wasted breath. **Courage is not the solution to your fear of young people.** The solution to fear is love— *"Perfect love drives out fear." (1 John 4:18)* To love young people requires that we gain a Christ-minded picture of them. With that picture in our minds, reaching out to young people with the love of Christ will be a natural and reasonable response. I dare say you'll even enjoy it!

That's the next chapter.

17

Renewed Pictures of Young People

In this chapter I will offer a new metaphor or picture of young people that will reduce your fear and increase your compassion for them. It is a biblical concept, but it is also the cry of our culture.

The Cry of the Culture

Been to a movie lately? Most young people have. Eighty percent of teenagers have seen a movie in the last 12 weeks.[5]

Movies are the most effective way that this culture tells its stories. Movies are art, but they're also business. Moviemakers study their audiences and then provide plots, pictures, music, and sounds that touch the hearts of those viewers who then talk to friends about what they saw and felt. If their words have impact, their friends will go see the movie, too. In other words, moviemakers know how to create evangelists by touching the heart of an audience. Their strategy is working.

---

[5] See http://www.valmorgan.com.au/au/audiences/demographics/age/ Though many of the characters and movies may be unknown to you, the young people around you will know nearly all of them.

We would be wise to take note of their strategy. To do that, read through the following characters from popular films.

- Harry Potter
- Batman
- Superman
- Spiderman
- Ironman
- Will Turner of "Pirates of the Caribbean"
- The Baudelaire children of the Liminy Snicket film and book series
- Indigo Montoya of "The Princess Bride"
- Truman of "The Truman Show"
- Buddy in "Elf"
- Luke Skywalker
- Alcjandro in "The Mask of Zorro"
- All of the X-Men
- Wolverine
- Will of "Good Will Hunting"
- Maverick in "Top Gun"
- Lily Owens in "The Secret Life of Bees"
- The Pevensie children in "The Lion, the Witch, and the Wardrobe"
- Benjamin Button
- Eliot in "ET"
- Wall-E
- August Rush
- Margaret in "The Proposal"
- Lucy in "While You Were Sleeping"
- The Boy Scout in "UP"
- Bambi
- Snow White
- Cinderella
- Lewis in "Meet the Robinsons"

- Lilo in "Lilo and Stitch"
- Aladdin
- Belle in "Beauty and the Beast"
- Tarzan
- Buzz Lightyear in "Toy Story"
- Peter Pan
- The Children in "Escape to Witch Mountain"
- Ariel in "The Little Mermaid"
- James in "James and the Giant Peach"
- Nemo in "Finding Nemo"
- Simba of "The Lion King"
- Mighty Joe Young
- Hiccup in "How to Train your Dragon"
- Michael Oher in "The Blind Side"
- Flint Lockwood in "Cloudy with a Chance of Meatballs"
- The three girls in "Despicable Me"
- Lyra in "The Golden Compass"
- Eragon Hawkeye in "Last of the Mohicans"
- Matt Murdock in "Daredevil"
- Becky Sharp in "Vanity Fair" (2004)
- Peter in "Finding Neverland"

What does each of those characters have in common?

The answer: **Every character listed is an orphan**, or a partial orphan (separated from at least one parent).

Why So Many Orphans?

The Orphan Hero is not new in storytelling. It is a common motif in ancient literature around the world. On a practical level, writers use orphans to keep things simple. Orphans have no meddling parent to complicate the plot or to rescue them, but on an emotional level, orphans touch our hearts. Obviously we are naturally sympathetic to vulnerable orphans out of pity for them. We all hoped Dorothy would get home to Auntie Em or that Little Orphan Annie or Pollyanna would find a real home.

But why so many orphans now? Dr. Chap Clark, professor of youth, family, and culture at Fuller Theological Seminary, spent a school year as a substitute teacher in a high school. Following that year, he wrote his observations in his book titled *Hurt*.[6] His central conclusion: Many young people feel abandoned by the adult world. In other words, they feel orphaned to some degree. Consequently, young people do not merely feel compassion for the Orphan Hero on the screen; they identify with him. They not only pity him, they share his fear and ultimately his triumph. Those movies touch young people's hearts in a special way.

Hollywood knows this. Nearly every Disney protagonist is an orphan. Disney writer Christopher Vogler wrote an influential book[7] extrapolating his take on Joseph Campbell's mythology studies, which were influenced by Carl Jung's archetypal theories in psychology.

Jung believed the pictures in our minds are the residue of foundational images passed to us from lower forms of life through the evolutionary process. According

---

[6] Clark, C. (2004). *Hurt: Inside the World of Today's Teenagers.* Grand Rapids, MI: Baker Academic.

[7] Vogler, C. (1998). *The writer's journey: Mythic structure for writers.* Michael Wiese Productions.

Vogler, Christopher (1992). The Writer's Journey: Mythic Structure for Storytellers and Screenwriters. Studio City, CA.: Michael Wiese Productions

to Jung and Campbell, man developed his gods and his mythologies of religions from those images.

I would agree that we have shared images in our minds. We do resonate with certain plots, characters, and scenes that echo through the world's religions, but I would assert that those are a result of our creation in the image of God, that God invented us; we didn't invent Him. God wired those images into our minds at Creation. They are twisted by sin, but something in us still hopes that our lives and the characters around us will be resonant with them.

In my opinion, the influence of Campbell and Vogler on screenwriters has made movie plots more formulaic, but the formula works because the Orphan Hero touches the part of us that feels separated from our Father, the part that feels we were made for something special but are missing the parental figure that will lead us to it.

The Orphan in Scripture

Moses was separated from his parents. Lot, Joash, Mephibosheth, and Esther were orphans. Lamentations 5:3 complains, *"We have become orphans and fatherless,"* but Psalm 68 says, *"God is father to the fatherless."* In the Old and New Testaments, He calls His people to the care of orphans. God is the Defender of the orphan and is against those who harm the orphan.

But there is a larger story that all men are part of, the larger meta-narrative of the Bible: we are and were the orphans. Mankind was separated from our Father by our sin, hoping to be reunited. Jesus was the only begotten Son of the Father, but we who are in Christ are now adopted sons and daughters. Like the prodigal son, we hoped to return as a servant, but He embraced us as His children. Romans 8 unveils this adoption by the Father through our faith in Christ.

All of this adds a new facet to our portrait of the Gospel: When Christ moved toward us, we were resurrected, freed, extracted, and empowered, but more than that—we were made children. We do not merely imitate Christ in His movement toward others; we can now imitate Him in our relationship with the Father. By the Second Adam we are restored to a position better than that of the First Adam. We don't merely walk with God as His creations; His Spirit dwells in us, and we are sons and daughters.

A New Picture of Young People

In light of these biblical and cultural considerations, I offer to you and your church a new picture of young people. They are not animals or foreigners or locked spaces; they are not to be feared, avoided, or kept at a distance.

Young people around you are orphans, separated from their Father, hoping to be heroes, but not knowing how to connect to that Father or how to be that hero. They are scared and alone, longing to know the full love and blessing of their Father, to find a community that feels like family, a purpose that focuses their lives, and a destiny worth living for.

We who are in Christ can connect them to all of that, but we need fresh eyes to look past the hair, the dress, and the behavior, past their attitudes and defenses, and past our own fears. We must see them through God's eyes with the mind of Christ.

As orphans, their beastly or foreign ways are not malicious. Their handshakes, tattoos, or piercings do not necessarily reflect a lack of integrity or respect for the cultural norm; it reflects a lack of knowledge or lack of value for an adult culture in which they don't feel welcomed.

That surly look they turn on you is not rooted in hatred; it is rooted in fear. If they don't know how to interact with adults, they will avoid them. They have been trained by life, as you have, to keep people at a distance to avoid disappointment and pain.

In their wandering off, they hope to be found. In their abandonment, they hope to be adopted. In their anger, they hope to be calmed, but hope deferred makes the heart sick. (Proverbs 13:12)

They still hope someone older and wiser will teach them how to be an adult, that someone will care enough to see their need for spiritual parenting, and get close enough to see the potential in them to be unlikely but powerful heroes for the Kingdom. That's where you and the other adults in your church come in.

In the next section, we will compare our current perception of adult roles in the lives of young people to a renewed picture.

Part Five:
Adult Roles in
Young Lives

18

Current Picture:
The Old Guard

My family visited Arlington National Cemetery several years ago. We had joined the current of chattering tourists shuffling past the eternal flame at JFK's grave and up the hill to a set of iron gates where a sign welcomed us:

> *Welcome to Arlington National Cemetery,*
> *Our Nation's Most Sacred Shrine.*
> *Please Remember:*
> *These Are Hallowed Grounds.*

Inside the gates is an amphitheater facing a marble monument that honors the unidentified dead from past wars. No matter the weather or the hour, members of the Old Guard repeat a clearly defined and unchanging ritual, steeped in symbolism and tradition. Visitors learn very quickly that these men don't simply guard the Tomb of the Unknowns; they guard the tone of the place. There is no room for frivolity here. No sarcasm, no taunting, no "let's try to make the guard laugh." As the sign says, this is hallowed ground.

If visitors to the site demonstrate any behavior in the area that would seem inappropriate for this hallowed ground, the members of the Old Guard will call them down with an authoritative and practiced script. The thrust of their message is simple: "In this place, you will not forget!"

It all started in 1926 when complaints came from soldiers who saw tourists using the monument as a picnic table. Soldiers were assigned to protect the site from disrespect. Soon a series of rituals evolved: 21 steps, pause for 21 seconds, turn and repeat, etc. These guards come from the Army's 3rd U.S. Infantry Regiment, known as the Old Guard.

A position in the Old Guard at the Tomb of the Unknowns is a high honor. The sixth line of their creed declares their standard: Perfection. Though their weapons are Vietnam-era rifles with an obsolete wooden stock and no magazine in place, the Old Guard marches on. There are no picnics here. Ironically, despite all their guarding, the monument is decaying, cracking, and in need of repair.

So I find it interesting that many pastors speak of the Old Guard to refer to aging members who ritually guard their church from change, using outdated, impotent efforts, and scolding those who seem to have forgotten what it all means.

Some readers may be hoping this next paragraph is the one I use to attack the Old Guard and send them on their way, humiliated; the one you can wave under their noses next Sunday, and say, "See, I told you! I am right! This guy wrote it in a book! I win!"

If that's true, I am grieved. That attitude does not represent the mind of Christ. Those older members are a gift to your church. If you perceive them to be a barrier to the future of your church, I beg you to gain a new picture of them. They are not barriers. They represent faithfulness and potential! They warn the next generation in solemn tones not to forget the value of what has gone on before. They may sound angry or resentful, but the responses were developed because those members care so deeply.

I suspect some Old Guard readers are puffing out their chests at this point, feeling that they have an ally who will support their strategies to guard the Church from change, someone to whom they can write nice letters saying, "Thanks for putting the whippersnappers in their places."

But that is not the mind of Christ either.

We must stop thinking of ourselves or others as the Old Guard. The church building is not the Tomb of the Unknown Savior; it is a place for the celebration of life and new birth authored by a God we know. We are not charged in Scripture with guarding a sacred site. We are charged with spreading a message of God's love and salvation through Christ Jesus.

Yes, the message of the Church is, "Do not forget the price Jesus paid on the cross," but it is so much more than that. What about resurrection? What about forgiveness? What about joy? What about love? What about community? What about Jesus' prayer that we would be one? (John 17) These are also important in our message. These joyous components rise out of His most serious sacrifice, but our attempts to prolong the solemnity and grief over the death of Christ without regard to His resurrection and ascension are not reflective of the mind of Christ. Paul's response and that of the early Church is clear and consistent: "Rejoice!"

We need to replace the image of the Old Guard with a new picture.

19

A Renewed Picture of Adult Roles

If you want to learn about Arlington National Cemetery, don't ask the Old Guard on duty. They don't see it as their job to be guides. Their minds are set on guarding. However, there are guides available for tours. These guides simply show people the way to walk. They welcome the newcomers, preview the journey, and offer stories and information along the way. Like the guards, they care about the place and its meaning, but, unlike the guards, they connect to the people. They are not symbolic or ritualistic; they are relational; they walk with the people as they teach them.

But those guards care more and know more about the place than anyone. They are required to study the history and the layout of the place. I imagine they could make wonderful guides. **So . . . what if the guards in your church became the guides?** Who else cares so deeply and knows so much? If those who thought of themselves as guards were willing to step from their posts to share their wisdom and passion with young people, your church would change. More importantly, lives would change, both young and old.

If young people are Orphans, they need guides; first, to move toward them as Christ moved toward us; and, secondly, to guide them toward their Father. Hopefully, those adults come with a measure of wisdom gained from experience in the faith, so the picture I offer in this chapter is not simply guide, but Wise Guide.

Wise Guides

Young people need Wise Guides. Without them, young people are delaying their entrance into adulthood. They marry later and have children later. Adolescence has expanded beyond the teen years into the twenties. I would suggest that young people are simply scared to grow up, because they've not been shown how to do adulthood well. They hope to meet trustworthy, older people who will leave their safe positions and safe routines. They hope to meet people who will imitate Christ in their movement toward them and show them how to walk.

Every adult believer I've met who is thriving in the faith can point to Wise Guides from the early and middle parts of their stories. Some have one Wise Guide; some have many. For some it was a couple that took them in or led a small group. For some it was a parent. For some it was a grandparent or relative. For others it was a pastor or church leader.

This Wise Guide is the solution to the lonely cry of most young people's hearts: "Who will care enough to walk into this mess I call my life and give me some direction? Who will help me become the man or woman God designed me to be? Who will love me before I get there? Who will be mystical enough to connect me to something larger than this daily routine? Who will be strong enough to release me to find my destiny, rather than controlling me or trying to fix me?"

All of those questions are horribly selfish! That's normal for Orphans. Orphans are scared, which makes them focus on themselves (just like we do when we're scared), but the Wise Guide has a response to the Orphan's questions. His answer is not "I will satisfy your needs!" The Wise Guide simply says, "Follow me." And the questions that can be answered get answered along the way. Again we see evidence of what God is doing in the hearts of young people in the culture and in the Bible.

The Wise Guide in Movies

Young people hunger for Wise Guides. Moviemakers know this. Notice that almost every movie Orphan I listed in the previous chapter, encounters a Wise Guide at some point in the film.

The most popular example is Obi-Wan Kenobi, the Wise Guide to Luke Skywalker in the Star Wars films. Before Obi-Wan, Luke was a powerless, restless orphan, hoping for something more than his dusty life on Tatooine. Obi-Wan connects Luke to the power of the Force, teaches him about it, connects him to a new community, reveals Luke's identity as a Jedi knight, and ultimately releases him to his destiny. All of that eventually connects Luke to his real father (cue the breathing sound). As it's presented in Star Wars, it's not orthodox Christianity, but it is a pattern God created us to respond to. Something in us resonates with it.

First, the Wise Guide interrupts the disciple's boredom and restlessness. Then the Wise Guide protects, prepares, and guides the disciple. In the process, the Wise Guide connects the disciple to

- A new identity
- A new community
- A new power, and
- A life-purpose or destiny larger than himself.

Ultimately, the Wise Guide releases his follower to move toward his destiny and his eventual promotion to Wise Guide for the next generation. Without that guidance, young people react against their immediate circumstances with foolishness, anger, and fear.

The popularity of the following characters underlines the hunger in young people to have a Wise Guide. Notice the pattern from above played out in each example:

Harry Potter

Harry Potter is a frustrated, neglected Orphan, living under the stairs in a relative's home after the Evil One killed his parents. Hagrid, a not-so-wise, but well-meaning giant, walks into Harry's life, says, "C'mon, Harry," and takes him from his miserable existence to

Diagon Alley. There Hagrid equips Harry and sends him off to a school where Harry joins a new community, learns new power, and learns of his identity as a powerful wizard. He has other Wise Guides along the way through the seven books that have outsold the Bible since their publication. Eventually Harry is released to defeat the Evil One himself, which, interestingly, requires his own death and resurrection.

James T. Kirk

In the 2009 movie *Star Trek*, the writers made sure that James T. Kirk, (the strong, capable leader of the Enterprise that my generation grew up with) loses his father in the first five minutes, placing him on a path to become an angry, troubled rebel.

Kirk grows up a frustrated, purposeless under-achiever, until Captain Pike, one of his Wise Guides, invites him to join the Academy. There Kirk connects to a new community, finds new power (The Enterprise), and gains a new identity as its captain. Later, when all seems lost, Kirk encounters Spock, another Wise Guide, who reconnects him to his community and his destiny.

Frodo Baggins

Frodo Baggins is a restless Orphan living in a comfortable but relatively boring shire until the wise wizard Gandalf interrupts Frodo's life and leads him on a quest. Gandalf connects Frodo to new power in the Ring, and a new community called the Fellowship of the Ring. Eventually Gandalf must release Frodo to find the path that will fulfill his destiny as the Ring-bearer.

There are many other Wise Guides from literature and film:

- Arthur had Merlin.
- Mowgli of *The Jungle Book* had Bagheera.
- Batman had Alfred.
- The X-Men had Charles Francis Xavier.
- Nemo had Gill, an older fish who sees him not as an undersized youngster with a bad fin, but as the perfect hero to initiate their escape from the fish tank.
- In the *Mask of Zorro*, Alexandro meets Zorro who teaches him the skills and values he needs to become the new Zorro (his new identity).
- Maverick of *Top Gun* meets a friend of his deceased father, a hard-nosed instructor who sees his potential and guides him toward greatness and trust.
- Sandra Bullock's orphaned character is reconnected to a family by the wise friend of the family in *While You Were Sleeping,* and the same reconnection occurs in her more recent film, *The Proposal*, spurred on by the grandmother.

For some, Wise Guides are adoptive parents:
- Spiderman has Aunt May.
- Superman has Ma and Pa Kent.
- Anne Shirley has the Cuthberts at Green Gables.

For other film characters, their Wise Guides are a birth-parent.
- Forrest Gump had his mother, who passes on bits of wisdom that help steer the course of his life.

Though the Wise Guide may be involved on an ongoing basis, the role may come in a single moment, as in this Disney scene:

Bambi's mother is dead. Bambi now lies wounded and exhausted in the path of the forest fire, ready to lie passively and die, until his father walks in and commands him, "Get up! Bambi! Get up!" Bambi gets up and follows the wise stag to safety and adulthood.

Often a Wise Guide sacrifices greatly for his follower, sometimes even his life. In Gran Torino, a fatherless Asian boy learns from a wise (but grumpy) Clint Eastwood character, who gives strength, wisdom, a car, and eventually his life for the orphaned boy, who he first saw as an alien.

The Wisdom of Wise Guides

Most Wise Guides in film have flaws or weaknesses, but they have moral foundations and good intentions. They may have gained their wisdom from hurt or wounds in the past, which may make them reluctant to engage with the young follower at first. When they move toward the orphaned young person, it often reopens their old wounds for new pain, but they gain a more complete healing.

These Wise Guides may be shy or emotionally distant at first. They may be selective in who they talk to, or simply quiet, which can make them intimidating to younger people, who may avoid them, causing the Wise Guide to believe they do not want a relationship.

Once in a relationship, Wise Guides are *not* rescuers. They may protect the Orphan Heroes from death or temptation, but they do not control them or guard them from the natural consequences of foolishness, nor do they punish their followers or withdraw relationship for mistakes. They use mistakes to teach their followers and demonstrate their commitment to them.

Guiding Principles

Wise guides are not just wise; they are guides. Though they may appear to be static or wandering when they encounter the orphan, they either have or quickly develop a plan and a direction. Able to see the potential in the Orphan, Wise Guides arrive to support and to lead the youngster toward his destiny. They steadily and incrementally prepare the Orphan for that destiny, though the follower is often unaware of the intentionality of the process. The wax-on/wax-off sequence in *The Karate Kid* is a classic example.

I offer those movie examples as evidence that young people, who make up the majority of theater audiences, hunger for Wise Guides, but clearly, our faith is not founded on the imitation of movie characters, but on the model of Jesus, our Wise Guide.

20

The Ultimate Wise Guide

The clearest example of Jesus as the Wise Guide involves the discipleship of Peter. Though Peter is not an orphan as far as we know, he was separated from his Father by sin. He was an uneducated, relatively powerless fisherman called Simon, living in a quiet village, until Jesus walked by and said to him, "Follow Me."

Simon follows, and in doing so gains a new identity as Peter, the rock on which Christ would build His Church. He gains knowledge, a new community with the other disciples, and receives new power from the Holy Spirit. Even after he betrays Jesus, Peter is forgiven and released into his destiny as a fisher of men, a feeder of sheep, and a changer of history, who became a Wise Guide for others.

Guided, Called to Guide

We know that we are designed to be in relationship with God, our Father. When that relationship was broken by Adam's sin, our design did not change, therefore, apart from Christ, we carried a profound sense of abandonment. We were Orphans, hoping a Wise Guide would interrupt our lives. Now we who are in Christ have the mind of Christ, which stirs compassion for the young people's abandonment, and which compels us to move toward them in imitation of Christ. As Wise Guides, we are not saviors, but we know where He can be found, and, by His Grace and Spirit at work in us, our lives can illustrate His truth and love to those around us.

Our Wise Guide left His safe place and moved toward us in love and wisdom as Emmanuel, saying, "Follow Me!" After a time, He sends us out, saying, "Feed My sheep." He adopted us and now bids us to demonstrate His love by adopting others.

The Opportunity of "I'm not getting fed."

Too often mature adults become stagnant in their faith, complaining, "I'm just not getting fed." The speaker typically does not mean it as an accusation, but pastors take it as such, which may blind them to the opportunity it signals. **"I'm not getting fed"** usually means that the individual has reached a point in his Christian life that requires a shift in his source of growth.

Early on in our faith, we grow by receiving from others—instruction, wisdom, sermons, and teachings. At some point, God brings us to a place where teachings and sermons seem stale and tasteless. If we complain about the pastor or the church, we stagnate, but if we recognize that God has brought us to that place where we now grow by giving to others, we will flourish in our faith. Not getting fed means it is time to feed others. Like Peter, we were called to follow and learn, but there comes a point where we must feed His sheep. For a few that means formal teaching and preaching. For the rest of us, it means becoming Wise Guides to younger people around us.

Our Response

Remember that "pack" of young people lingering in front of your house? How might you respond differently if you see them now as Orphans? How might you respond differently now that you know they are **hoping** a Wise Guide will interrupt their dull lives and connect them to a community, a power, and a destiny?

They are not animals or aliens. They need us! They hope for us, and we are much more than the inadequate bumblers we perceive ourselves to be. We were designed, prepared, and called to go toward them as a dim reflection of Jesus. In that humble movement, we carry with us His Spirit to resurrect, to adopt, and to empower them. In Christ, we bring light, hope, and direction to their lives. Our bumbling simply reminds us that we need a Savior, but we must not forget His Spirit lives in us.

Their Response

When our movement toward them provides young people with a dim reflection of that loving swoop of Jesus Christ, they will respond. They are wired for it. At some point, the reflections we offer will make connections, and old corrupted circuits will start to smoke. For some, it will smell like life; for others, it will reek of death. (2 Corinthians 2:15-16) But they will respond! For those to whom it is life, we continue to be Wise Guides. We will see great things happen in their lives, and in ours. For the others who reject our movement, we grieve and pray, but at no point do they become the enemy.

Part Six:
The Church

21

Old Pictures of the Church

When a portion of your congregation sees the need for Wise Guides in the lives of the young and moves toward them in imitation of Christ, your church will begin to change— in good ways! It happens slowly and naturally as hearts are turned and as relationships build across generations. Fear decreases; faith and love grow; and your church changes. It's glorious to watch!

In one church it started with Linda. Linda is a single woman who didn't particularly care for kids. But day after day she drove past the neighborhood kids, and eventually God wore her down. She approached them and became a Wise Guide for them. Eventually she brought them to her church where those kids joined a new community, found a new identity in Christ, and experienced new power. I was honored to be present on a Sunday morning when one of "Linda's kids" was baptized.

These days they won't all fit into her car. The church sends a van to her neighborhood to pick them all up, but the best part is they're not "Linda's kids" anymore. Linda's church is beginning to see them as "our kids." Their picture of young people is changing. Their picture of their role in the lives of young people is changing. As those pictures of young people and their role in their lives are renewed, they have realized that the pictures that organize their thinking about their church require renewing as well. Like many congregations, they think with pictures that do not reflect the mind of Christ.

Old Picture 1: The Church as a Club with Benefits for Members

Consider these comments overflowing from the hearts of members of churches:

"I don't have to work in the nursery anymore. ***I've paid my dues***."

"You have to be a ***member*** before you can do that."

"Some folks just don't ***belong*** here."

"Excuse me, these are ***our seats***."

"Kids just ***don't belong*** in here. They disrupt the service."

In the hearts and minds of these speakers, their church is a club that offers benefits for members. The pictures include membership, belonging, being "in" the club, and the expectation of benefit from their investment in it. Those pictures do not reflect the mind of Christ.

We go to a club for the benefits it offers the members. It is not a place for sacrifice. The club provides the membership with relationships that share a common interest and perhaps a place to avoid the noise of the rabble who are not allowed in. The club hires people to do the lesser jobs, so that members can enjoy the place. Over time, Christians with a club mentality see themselves as God's elite on the inside.

If we think of the Church as a club, the goal of church leadership is to ensure that members pay their fees, to ensure they behave appropriately, and to ensure maintenance of the club's facilities. The leadership also offers weekly "services" to the members, who evaluate the club based on the pleasure and value they receive from those services.

Outsiders do not feel particularly welcomed at clubs. Imagine you are outside an Elk's Lodge or a country club. Do you feel free to walk in? Usually not. Generally there is a gate or gatekeeper on duty to monitor comings and goings. Young people are generally ignored or excluded until they are of age and offer clear signals they have accepted the values embraced by the club.

Picture 2:
Church as a School for Christians

If a church values Christian education and discipleship, it must be careful to encourage all of her disciples to become relational disciplers. Otherwise, that church may begin to resemble a school for Christians. In a school, the responsibility of discipleship falls on a few teachers who are respected but held at a distance, away from and above the crowd. Attenders begin to believe that knowledge acquired from formal teaching will solve life's problems and that life skills will naturally emerge in proportion to that knowledge.

Schools also place a high value on conformity to behavior and ideas. The motivations and outcomes often result from some overt or implied grading system. Those with the most knowledge and best behavior feel the most welcomed, and students may feel a sense of competition for the top spots with the teacher. Lower achievers may feel overlooked, or even shamed. They may leave.

In a school, the primary goal is the transfer and measurement of knowledge, rather than development of character or relationships, so being right becomes more important than being loving. When we reduce Christianity to education and knowledge, we plant seeds of pride and fear in our disciples. Students who excel in learning thrive. Those who don't may learn that asking questions simply reveals what they do not know, so they may become more guarded. Churches that are perceived as schools have lots of class time and are organized in efficient ways, placing students in developmentally appropriate classes hoping to efficiently target the ignorance in age-specific or need-specific groups. When class sizes (the number of people a particular teacher is responsible for) become too large, teachers get overwhelmed or tired. Students become reluctant to invite friends to join. Growth stalls.

The Church is not meant to be perceived primarily as a school. Certainly we cannot devalue biblical teaching, and there are essential educational components to the Church's ministry, but the intellectual preparation of the disciple is not the primary task of the Church. Scripture is clear that knowledge puffs us up (1 Corinthians 8:1), and 1 Corinthians 13:2 warns us *"If I have . . . all knowledge . . . but have not love, I am nothing."*

Current Picture 3:
Church as a Performance

If I see church as a performance, I go to church; I watch, then I critique, or I promote.

"The pastor has preached better sermons than that one."

"I thought the soloist was off her game this morning."

"That was a good service."

"We are effective and efficient with our ministry resources"

'We have a good youth ministry! Lots of smoke and lights!"

"He puts me to sleep with his sermons."

"You should come to our service sometime. It's great!"

Our children listen from the back seat, as we drive home evaluating the performance of all the players of the Sunday service. We treat our church as if it were the Cubs (we're loyal, but our expectations are low) or the Yankees (we dare anyone to beat our lineup week-in and week-out). If the services hit a slump, we grow restless. Constant negative evaluations of the Sunday performance may send us looking for a better show or a new star player.

If our church is a performance, we may invite the unchurched to the services, rather than to a relationship with Christ. We assume that if they enjoy the services, they will meet Christ eventually. It may happen, but it may be a cowardly and dangerous assumption, and that thinking is not reflective of the mind of Christ. Your church service is not a performance to be judged.

Other Old Pictures

There are several other pictures we use to conceptualize our churches.

The Church as a Service Station for My Life

With this picture in our mind's gallery, we say things like . . .

"I'm just hoping to get a spiritual tune-up."

"I just need some work done in my heart."

"I didn't get much out of their service."

"I come to get what I need to make it through the week."

"I come here to get my life fixed."

In Western culture, most church folks believe the goal of their staff of experts is to fix and maintain our lives; staff gets paid to make things run well for us. If they do not handle the problem, we get grumpy and complain about their service. In response, pastors may begin to focus on fixing the broken, rather than equipping the saints to do the ministry of the church.

If they don't provide good services, we may go elsewhere. We take our need to the experts at some other place, and let them attend to it. We begin to see the "service" not as our service to God and the community, but as what the professionals of the Church give our lives. Again, this is not the mind of Christ for our Church.

The Church as a Military/Mission Outpost

When churches speak of their "mission," some tend to think in military metaphors, which may cast outsiders as the enemy, pressing the Church into a defensive posture, which makes us offensive to many outsiders.

The "outpost" is a defensive site in a larger offensive. It is a temporary base from which attacks are carried out in a larger strategy against the enemy. An outpost is not a place you commit to for the rest of your life. It is a temporary station where you are a foreigner surrounded by a foreign culture. We do not view an outpost as home, not a place to settle in and persist.

At this point, some readers will begin to make connections and say, "But we ***are*** just passing through here. This is not our home; our home is in glory, and we are aliens here in this outpost called Earth."

True! And in that sense the Church may well be an outpost, but I do not believe it is an effective image around which we should organize our thinking. It does not translate well to the community outside the Church, and war metaphors do not motivate the Church to go out in love.

Even the military leaders in the Afghanistan conflict are abandoning their outpost mentality in favor of moving troops into villages to guard and serve the village, to build relationships, rather than remaining safely on the hill above the village and occasionally making intrusive and disruptive forays into it.

Rather than missions into the culture, we're the ones who are to be imitating the movement of Christ toward the people, setting aside our safe places, and entering into the suffering of Christ and of others, so that others may share in His resurrection.

The Church as a Temple or a Sanctuary

In some congregations, the church is the building. Coming into the sanctuary is equated with coming into the presence of God. The building is often a place where we "call down" the presence of God or invoke God to "show up" or "welcome Him," but those images are not theologically or biblically sound.

The veil in the Temple split after the death of Christ on the cross. The Holy Spirit was released in a new way from the confines of the Holy of Holies and poured into the lives of the believers on Pentecost. Consequently, we bring the Holy Spirit with us when we go to church. Additionally, we bring the Holy Spirit with us to no less a degree when we go to school, or to work, or to a party. His presence is with us all week, so the building we gather in is of little consequence to God.

That's blasphemy to the folks who see the sanctuary of their church as a special place of God's presence, a place where we say,

"We don't do that in church."

"Remember, you are in the house of God."

"This is a church! You shouldn't talk that way!"

"I can't believe she came to church dressed like that!"

But I find nothing in Scripture that requires my behavior in church to be better than my behavior outside of it, nor any suggestion that I can behave more poorly outside of church than in. We are called to be followers of Christ all week, not just at the church building. When the pictures in our minds free God from the building, we can more deeply envision that *we* are the sacred place where He has chosen to live.

Your church building is not a temple of the Holy Spirit. You are.

The Church as a Corporation

With the rise of the megachurch, the role of the pastor as CEO, and the leadership models based on secular models, some churches have become more like corporations. The leadership may begin to focus on the health and growth of the organization rather than the people in it.

If we are too organizational, ministry can become something we do to people rather than what happens in relationships as we learn to love well. Church leaders and members that think with this picture spend more time in preparation for the Sunday service than in relationships with other congregants. Admittedly, this is a complex point: Every group requires some organizational aspects, but to reach young people, the focus in most churches must grow more relational.

The Church leaders I've met are goodhearted folks. They want to organize communities of people, to focus them on significant and godly purposes, but leaders face special temptations. They learn early that Church leadership can be painful. People leave. People fail. People grumble. People bite. People betray. Many pastors grow discouraged or depressed, and the corporate model provides a tempting refuge. It allows leaders to develop a distance from the people, seeing them as consumers of the corporate products, but that is not the mind of Christ. Not for the Church, nor for the leader.

I point out this temptation, not to accuse pastors, but to allow you to understand that they may distance themselves for good reasons, for their own safety or sanity. Knowing that may allow you to pray differently for them, or give you new compassion for them, or it may encourage you to become a safe and encouraging relationship for them.

Coming Up

In the next chapter, I offer a renewed picture to replace these current pictures of the Church. I pray it will erase any offense I may have caused in presenting these, that it will increase both the love of the members and the effectiveness of your church at reaching and keeping young people.

22

A New Picture of the Church

"There's an old man at the door!" At my cousin's announcement, we all got quiet. It was Sunday afternoon. My extended family was gathered in the front room of my mother's childhood home on the family farm, the site of reunions and gatherings for generations. Strangers don't just show up there, unless they have had trouble or are looking for it. Whatever the reason, an old man was at the door, and our precious family time felt interrupted.

My cousin let him in. A stooped, white-haired gentleman, easily in his 80s, shuffled into the room where we were gathered. He took his time to look around the room, but when he saw my mother, he said gently, "Hello, Ann." Then to my aunt. "Hello, Louise . . . I'm Bud."

My mom jumped up and hugged him. My aunt stood up as fast as her knees would let her, and soon there were introductions and handshakes and hugs.

The old man at the door was not a threat to us; he was not an interruption; he was family, an uncle we'd not seen in decades. Instantly he was one of us. He brought his wife in from the car, and she was family too. We made room for them, and they joined in the storytelling. The noise and the laughter were back. It was a celebration again, even better than before. Later, as they left, we took pictures together, they were hugged again, and then they were missed.

Notice the shift in the images within our minds:

When we pictured an "old man at the door," we were all cautious and irritated that he interrupted our family time. When we saw him as family, we were delighted that Uncle Bud was there. He was the same person the whole time, but the picture of him in our brains changed. The fear and irritation melted away. We sacrificed our seats for him and his wife. We wanted them to feel at home. No, more than that—they *were* at home.

Certainly thousands of churches want guests to feel at home, but few of them fully embrace the depth of this family image and its potential impact on our behavior. With that episode in mind, I want to offer you a new biblical picture that will renew your thinking about church and resonate in the soul of a generation that feels abandoned and orphaned.

The Church is a Family

Seeing the new picture some may grumble, "Old news! Everybody knows the Church is supposed to be like a family!"

Maybe that's the problem! The Church is not supposed to be "like a family"; it *is* a family. Rather than acting like a family, we would do well to grasp the reality that we *are* family. To start repainting and renewing our perception of the Church, let's take a fresh look at God's design of the family.

Biblical Family

Family is foundational in God's design. God refers to Himself as the God of Abraham, Isaac, and Jacob, recalling three generations of a single family. His covenant with Abraham extended through the generations of that family. Though the Hebrew nation was divided into 12 tribes, their larger identity came from Jacob (Israel), their common ancestor, so when we speak of the 12 tribes of Israel, we refer not to 12 groups in a single nation-state, but to descendants of Jacob through his 12 sons. A family.

Therefore, the grumbling mob that left Egypt and wandered in the desert was a single family, not a nation of strangers. They were related by blood and by a family covenant that God had made with their ancestors.

In the same way, David did not become king of a territory; he became the patriarch of a single family. The Hebrew men in his armies were from the same family and fought for family land and family homes, not a geo-political organization. For them, circumcision was more than a reminder of the covenant they had with God; it was a family mark that identified members as "us" and not "them."

The Ark of the Covenant held their family's heirlooms, given to them by God. The Temple was their family's gathering spot and their family worship center. The site had family roots back to Abraham. The city of Jerusalem became their shared hometown, their reunion site where they reminded the family of its heritage, including Passover, the night when their ancestors were spared by God because of the blood of the lamb.

Their tithes helped support the priests, who were their cousins, not strangers running a religious organization. The Scriptures recorded the history of their family and God's faithfulness to it. In those genealogies that make us roll our eyes, they trace their relatives back to their father Abraham. The Scriptures connect them as a family with a shared history, shared covenant, and shared blood.

Jesus' Repainting of Family Pictures

Family was central to the Jewish faith, but in the Old Testament we rarely see God portrayed as their "Father." (Hosea 11:1; 2 Samuel 7:14; 1 Chronicles 17:13; 1 Chronicles 22:10; Psalm 89:27) Perhaps for the Jews, the role of father was too intimate to associate with the I AM, but Jesus changed that. By all Gospel accounts, He repeats the picture of God as a father, not just "My Father," but also "your Father" in addressing the disciples, and *"Our Father"* in the opening of the Lord's Prayer. Paul reinforces the picture of God as Father, opening ten letters with this greeting: *"Grace and peace to you from God our Father."*

Additionally, Jesus recasts the way they saw God's family. Among the Pharisees, the fatherhood of Abraham seems to be a point of great pride. In Matthew 3, Jesus trivializes their importance as children of Abraham, *"And do not think you can say to yourselves, 'We have Abraham as our father.' I tell you that out of these stones God can raise up children for Abraham."*

As much as His attack seemed to devalue the role of Abraham, Jesus is more concerned with promoting the fatherhood of God. Later, in Matthew 23:8-9, Jesus warned His disciples with His references to brotherhood and fatherhood:

> *"But you are not to be called 'Rabbi,' for you have only one Master and you are all brothers. And do not call anyone on earth 'father,' for you have one Father, and He is in heaven."*

Then immediately afterward in verse 15, He attacks the Pharisees, questioning their parentage even more vehemently: *"Woe to you, teachers of the law and Pharisees, you hypocrites! You travel over land and sea to win a single convert, and when he becomes one, you make him twice as much **a son of hell** as you are."*

To paraphrase: "You are not sons of God! You are not even sons of Abraham; you are sons of hell, who are producing as your disciples double-strength sons of hell."

It is a stinging jab, and part of His repainting of the Jews' pictures of family. Being a son of Abraham was no longer enough. God's children were no longer those born of circumcised men who could trace their lineage to Jacob and beyond. It was anyone who believed in Him and followed Him by faith. This becomes still clearer in Mark 3 and elsewhere as He again reframed their picture of family:

> *20Then Jesus entered a house, and again a crowd gathered, so that He and His disciples were not even able to eat. 21When His family heard about this, they went to take charge of Him, for they said, "He is out of His mind." ... Standing outside, they sent someone in to call Him. 32A crowd was sitting around Him, and they told Him, "Your mother and brothers are outside looking for You."*

> 33"Who are My mother and My brothers?" He asked.
>
> 34Then He looked at those seated in a circle around Him and said, "Here are My mother and My brothers! 35Whoever does God's will is My brother and sister and mother."

The implications of that episode may disrupt our current perception of our Church. Those who value the sanctity of the nuclear family over their relationship to the Church may be pressed to broaden their definition of family. I assure you I am not devaluing the nuclear family, but neither will I devalue Jesus' willingness to value spiritual relationships as at least equal to family relationships. In anticipation of the impact of the waves He would cause in families, Jesus says,

> "I tell you the truth . . . no one who has left home or wife or brothers or parents or children for the sake of the kingdom of God will fail to receive many times as much in this age and, in the age to come, eternal life." (Luke 18:29-30)

Many times as much of what? Of what they left behind—home and family. When? In this age and in the age to come . . . now and in heaven. So if a man must leave his family for the Gospel, he gains a new home and a new family. Where is that family? It's your church, the Christians around you, and all believers on the earth. That's not grounds to leave an unbelieving spouse or to disown unsaved children, but it is grounds to take a fresh look at the relationships in your church.

The narrow Jewish frame around the family of Abraham that allowed the Jews to set their family apart from outsiders is obliterated after Peter begins to reach out to the uncircumcised Gentiles. As he defends his outreach to them in Acts 11, Peter, a Jew, is careful to use the word "brother" to refer only to Jews.

*"The Spirit told me to have no hesitation about going with them [Gentiles]. These six **brothers** [Jewish Christians] also went with me, and we entered the man's house."*

But by the time Paul is writing to the churches, he addresses all the followers of Christ as brothers whether Gentile or Jew. Additionally, the New Testament word for "disciple" (*mathetes*) is used more than 250 times in the Gospels and Acts, but it is NEVER used in the Epistles.

Why is that? How can a concept like discipleship that seems so central to the teaching of Jesus (*"Go and make disciples . . ."*) never appear in the Epistles?

From what I see in Scripture, the apostles and the early Church thought of one another using mental pictures of family. Between the beginning of Acts and the end of Revelation, the term "brother" is the most frequent address-word, used more than 230 times to refer to people in the Church.

Disciple (*mathetes*) carries with it the Greco-Roman connotations of the relationship of a schoolmaster and a student or apprentice.[8] If the early Christians were thinking in terms of family, *mathetes* is too formal an expression for them.

Likewise, when these early believers were *"sharing all things together,"* they were not thinking with a picture of a commune or socialism. They were family. What else would a family do? They were not going house to house as company. They were family, not **like** a family. They

---

[8] Wilkins, M. J. (1992). *Following the Master: discipleship in the steps of Jesus.* Zondervan. p. 72.

didn't say "brother" as an archaic, formal address to another church member. They meant "brother" with warmth, as in related by blood, sharing the same father, and at home in the same house. They had a sense of that connection to a degree that the Church must rediscover if we are to reach the next generation, which is starving for a community that will be a family to them.

More than Wise Guides

Additionally, this renewed picture of the Church as family stretches our picture of Wise Guides. In Galatians 3:23-26, Paul attempts to repaint the relational word-pictures by tracing our promotion or progression from prisoner to students under a stern tutor to children of our Father.

*"Before this faith came, we were held **prisoners** [phroureō = guarded to prevent escape] by the law, locked up until faith should be revealed. So the law **was put in charge** [paidagōgos—KJV uses "schoolmaster"; others use "tutor"] to lead us to Christ that we might be justified by faith. Now that faith has come, we are no longer under the supervision of the law. You are all **sons** of God through faith in Christ Jesus . . ."*

Paul uses the same words and imagery in 1 Corinthians 4:14-15, *"I am not writing this to shame you, but to warn you, as my dear **children**. Even though you have ten thousand **guardians** [paidagōgos = school-masters] in Christ, you do not have many **fathers**, for in Christ Jesus **I became your father** through the gospel."*

With this new broadening of the family, Paul is more than a Wise Guide to his disciples; he becomes their spiritual father. If we see churches as schools and adults as stern schoolmasters or guards rather than as spiritual mothers and fathers in the family of God, then we will not make lifelong disciples of Jesus Christ from this generation. We will see them leave after graduation.

If your congregation is going to keep its young people, the Church must see itself as a family and begin to conduct itself in that way, offering close, nurturing relationships **across generations**.

23

Across the Generations

In the theater of your mind, let this movie roll: (Fade in)

It's spring. A glorious day! You are working outside with your family. As the camera pulls back from your family, you realize this particular day is 2500 springs ago. It's about 500 B.C. in ancient Jerusalem. You're one of the priests rebuilding the foundation of the temple on the same site of the old temple, which was a really nice temple, but the Babylonians leveled it a while back.

Since it's your theater and your mind, you may choose whether you are an old priest who remembers that original temple, or a young priest who has no memory of it (though you've certainly heard the stories the old guys told).

No matter your choice or your age, you are excited to be part of this project, so you join in with the old and young folks, all working together to move the heavy foundation stones into place. Some are pulling. Some are pushing. Some measuring, and some supervising, but all are working together toward one goal: Build this thing!

On this particular spring day, the final foundation stone is laid in place, and a little celebration breaks out as recorded in the book of Ezra, Chapter 3—

"... *all the people gave a great shout of praise to the LORD, because the foundation of the house of the LORD was laid."*

But after this brief celebration, things get weird!

"But many of the older priests and Levites and family heads, who had seen the former temple, wept aloud when they saw the foundation of this temple being laid, while many others shouted for joy." (Ezra 3:11-12)

Notice that one moment you and all of the priests began to rejoice and worship together, but in the next moment the older priests (perhaps you) began to weep as they remember the glory of the former temple. Not sniffling or whimpering, this was sobbing—loud, messy, undignified wailing. Wow, they loved that old temple!

In the same moment, the younger priests begin to cheer, celebrating this new work God has for them with volume equal to that of the old guys' weeping. Linger here a moment while the echoes of the noise roll off in the distance, while you consider the situation.

Clearly this is odd. The older folks are looking back, remembering what was; the younger folks are looking forward, excited about what is to come; but all are reacting strongly—and very differently! One family divided along generational lines by their different perspectives on a single event. This scene depicts a recipe for division, an opportunity for anger and the separation of two generations. The two groups could argue, one side demanding that the young folks show some respect—the other complaining that the older folks need to get over it, stop living in the past, and join in the celebration. The young people could start work on a youth temple to avoid the awkwardness of the weepy, old priests, but the scene continues.

> *"No one could distinguish the sound of the shouts of joy from the sound of weeping, because the people made so much noise. And the sound was heard far away."*

As far as the people outside the worksite can tell, this is a picture of unity:

all are members of the same family of Israel;

all are living in the same moment and in the same place;

all are seeing the same rocks and the same foundation;

all are invested in the same project;

all are worshipping the same God, and

all are caring deeply and reacting with great volume and emotion.

All are creating one noise.

The cheerers did not win. The weepers did not win. They blended into one noise, and people far away heard it—one unified noise.

There is still the potential for division, but the glorious part of this movie in your mind is that it doesn't end here. Once the outbursts end, the book of Ezra explains that all the workers went back to work side by side and finished the job God gave them. One family built one temple—not a youth temple and an old folks temple— one Temple, for one family to worship one God, as He directed.

Our Ezra 3 Moment

We live in an Ezra 3 moment today: a time full of tensions between younger and older generations with different perspectives regarding the work before us. Depending on your church, the younger people may be bored, or they may be excited about what God is doing in their lives and communities. They cheer the new music and the new things happening in the Kingdom, while older members may look back wistfully or grieve the loss of what was their church.

But most churches are missing that singleness of purpose found in the family in Ezra 3. Today, the younger may scoff at the music or traditions of the older; the older may guard defiantly, seeing any change as loss or compromise, and refusing to lose more or compromise further. When we lost our single purpose, we accepted the market niches within the Church and attempted to satisfy all their needs.

We view the Church as one big compromise, not much to get excited about. Our attempts to please all the factions in music, liturgy, and programming are pleasing none. In response, we have avoided speaking the truth in love and ended up communicating less, expecting less, and hoping less.

Our modern picture of the generations in churches assumes that each slice of the demographic pie must be served on its own plate, but Jesus prayed in John 17 that we would be one as He and the Father are one. In other words, the unity in the followers of Christ should reflect the mystery and family of the Trinity. We should be so unified that it would be difficult to talk about any one of us without talking about the others.

But the way we think about unity among believers in our Church family and between churches in our cities, countries, and globally falls far short of what is in the mind of Christ. Much of what we consider unity may be merely a strong alliance between members of a particular faction against another faction, our "US" boundaried off from the competitive "THEM." It feels like unity within our alliance, but it may be a disguise for the sin and selfishness that rises from our unspoken demand for comfort. If we perceive our US to be above, better than, or more deserving or privileged than any THEM in the Church, it may be time to repent. Jesus' teaching offers no room for such attitudes between generations or denominations.

We live in an Ezra 3 moment. I pray we can picture the generations with the mind of Christ and build the Kingdom together. We need to replace our current picture of the Church as demographic slices or a loose collection of special-needs groups with a picture of family united around building the Kingdom of our Father.

But our family is different. That's the next chapter.

24

The Intentionally Adoptive Family

Almost any family would take in an orphaned baby left on its doorstep. The Penick family is different; they go looking for orphans. Like Hosea and Joseph, the Penicks' lives reflect God's truth to us. They offer a picture of God's family at its most powerful—when it is intentionally adoptive.

Scott and Suzi Penick have three fine, begotten children, but they decided to embrace the stranger as family. Consequently, they have adopted four more fine children—two young ones from China and two teenagers from Ukraine. They didn't look for the kids they needed; they prayerfully looked for the ones who needed them.

In the Penicks' heart for adoption, I see the heart of Christ and a vision of the Church. To paraphrase Philippians 2, they didn't consider comfort, ease, or an empty nest something to be grasped. They chose to release these things and go toward those who were not their own to make them their own. They made "them" part of their "us," and it has made a huge difference in the lives of those kids who will understand God's adoption of us, as discussed in Romans 8, not as a concept, but as reality. They've watched their family live it out.

The Penicks could easily say they can do no more, that they've done their part, but if you ask Scott Penick what he would do differently, his eyes will fill with tears, and he will say simply, "Artur."

Artur is a bright young man in Ukraine, stricken with significant cerebral palsy. He would wheel himself through the crowded orphanage to find quiet places where he could read. Artur was the one Scott couldn't adopt. He tried, but by the time the paperwork was done, Artur would have been over 18 and not adoptable.

Scott's soft heart reflects to me the heart and mind of Christ for young people—moving toward them to adopt them into the family of God, giving them a new identity as members of His family, a new purpose, a new life in a new community, no matter the cost, no matter the cultural differences, or the pain.

I'm not suggesting that you go overseas to adopt (though if God leads you that way, by all means, go for it). I am suggesting that our hearts should be willing to seek out those who feel orphaned or abandoned in your church or in your community. If we wait for them to come to our doorstep, we'll miss an opportunity. The Penicks illustrate the intentional and sacrificial adoption that we experience so generously from our Father. Now we can reflect the same to a culture of young people who feel orphaned.

The church that just wants young people to get saved will die, but the church that wants to move toward them, adopt them, and raise them in the family of God will prosper. Hurling the seeds of the Gospel at them may cause their hearts to become rocky ground. The young people around us may require that we get closer than is currently comfortable, in order to plant the Gospel in their hearts and care for its growth in them.

25

One Family Across the Generations

One Sunday afternoon in January 2001, as I sat in my office, I heard the muffled prayers of teenagers coming from the chapel beside my office. I thought, "Oh, how nice! Students are praying!"

Then I realized they were praying against me—loud prayers asking God to change my heart, to change my mind, to move me on to another church if I remained blind to what the Lord wanted me to do.

"Lord, open his eyes!" one chanted, and in response another would agree with a loud "Yes, Lord," which emboldened the original speaker to say it again and louder. They were getting more and more agitated. It was like a revival had broken out, and I was the blind, evil enemy they were praying against!

I sat alone and wondered, "How did I get here?"

I had arrived seven months earlier. We moved three weeks after my wife's last surgery for breast cancer, uprooted from the safe little church in which I'd grown up, where I served as the youth pastor to the finest little youth group in the world. My wife and I arrived at this big church where I was introduced as "One of the finest youth pastors in the nation."

We laughed at that. No one else did. Expectations were high among the adults, but the students hated me; I was turning their independent peer group into an intergenerational ministry with more adults and more parents in the room each week. Some of the parents didn't like the idea either. Some complained, "It'll never work."

I had expected resistance, so, as we cranked up in September, I promised we'd have a special meeting in January and evaluate how the new intergenerational thing was going.

"Until then," I said, "let's give it a shot."

It appeased the grumpy folks, but the January meeting had come fast, and now the original group of influential upperclassmen was organized in prayer, trying to get God on their side. As far as I could tell, it was working. I felt horribly alone, so I put on my jacket, left their supplications behind, and walked for a bit, wondering what it would be like to move again so soon.

An hour later, the big evaluation meeting started. We did our normal welcome, some announcements, and a few songs of worship. Then I started the discussion with a brief review of the fruit I had seen, but after four months I didn't have much clear evidence, so I stopped my nervous chattering and asked if anyone wanted to add their thoughts.

As I expected, all heads turned toward the most vocal and grumpiest of students in the group whose hand was already raised. I called on him and braced for the barrage.

He started, "Uh . . . earlier, we were praying . . . uh, praying against you, and all these changes you've made..."

I just smiled nervously, wondering why he was so hesitant.

". . . and it was really good to pray together, but then the adults came in . . ."

I was stunned. I had forgotten that my adult intercessory team would gather in the same chapel where those kids were praying. They had arrived just after I took my walk.

The vocal upperclassman continued, ". . . and they prayed with us, and it was really powerful when we were all together, so, uh, we've changed our minds. We think having more adults around is a good thing, and we should continue as we've been going."

And with that, the opposition to my crazy intergenerational ways ended. My heated opponents were now my strong allies. Young people began to welcome parents, and, sooner than we all expected, it felt normal for parents, other adults, and even younger siblings, to be there. The group grew as students and parents became ambassadors for it. It was wonderful.

I could take no credit for it. It was not my cleverness that got us to that point. It was the God of all generations working to turn the hearts of the fathers to the children and hearts of the children to the fathers (Malachi 4:5-6). I got to see it firsthand that Sunday night in 2001, and I'll never forget it. It was glorious! And I've seen it happen in church after church when adults have their minds renewed and are reminded that Jesus' desire is that we be one (John 17), and His design is that we be a family.

Part Seven: Implications and Applications

26

So What?

I avoid formulas and step-by-step recipes for Christian success. This will frustrate some readers who were hoping I would provide the clear answer for "What do I do now?"

I am enough of a mystic to trust that, if we are prayerfully approaching the mind of Christ and His Spirit lives in us, God will make the next steps clear for each of us in our particular settings. The components of this section are offered as springboards to launch individuals, small groups, and congregations into prayer, discussion, and action.

Pressing Past Barriers

Our fear of approaching young people seems like a physical barrier at times. It will paralyze us, if we are not careful. Seeing young people as Orphans in need of Wise Guides can reduce that fear, but it's normal to feel some nervousness about approaching them at first. There are several reasons.

Less than the Best

We all want the best for our young people and our children, but most are convinced that we're not the best thing for their spiritual growth: "The Youth Pastor is the expert; let him handle it."

But young people don't necessarily think they need the best person to guide them; they just want someone to do it. In Christ, we are each an essential part of an intentionally adoptive family that passes its heritage through the generations. In Christ we are indwelt by the Holy Spirit and function as the incarnation of Jesus Christ to one another. In that identity, we have the opportunity to carry good things to everyone we meet.

Our fear of anything less than perfection turns the Christian life into a high-wire walk—one misstep in any direction means great pain, so we grow paralyzed. That picture breeds fear. It is not the mind of Christ for our lives. We are the people who rejoice; we are the people who love. We are not called to a life of fear, so let the picture of life as a high-wire act die and consider seeing your life as surfing—where balance is still valued, but everyone ends up in the water at some point, and we come up laughing and grateful. Then we paddle back out and try again. It's tough to evangelize people to be high-wire walkers, but evangelizing surfers is easy: "Come on out. I'll teach you."

You don't have to be the best teacher; you simply have to show up with some wisdom to pass on.

Less than Adequate

Still, even if we get our pictures of them sorted out, we may be scared to approach young people because we believe we are inadequate to disciple them—and we're right! We are completely inadequate to transform their lives. Even those who have all the knowledge, the biblical principles, and the doctrine worked out cannot do what a young person requires. But when we walk by faith in love, God's Spirit works through us to do mighty things.

Realizing that we are inadequate is essential to our success as Wise Guides. Our inadequacy is not a hindrance; it is a gift from God. It reminds us that we are merely human, that we need a Savior. It keeps us tuned to the Holy Spirit and crying out to God for what we need and what our followers need.

Apart from Christ we can do nothing, but with Him all things are possible. So rather than letting our inadequacy stop us from discipling others, we can embrace it as perhaps the very thing that qualifies us to disciple them, because "His strength is made perfect in our weakness."

If we wait until we are strong, we will be tempted by self-reliance and pride, but if we accept inadequacy as a gift, we train our disciples that they too can do mighty things for the Kingdom now, not waiting until they are fully adequate.

Still there may be some apprehension.

The Opposite of Fear

Our culture encourages fear. It profits from fear. The message of the local TV news hour is simple: "Be afraid. Criminals, disease, and poverty are right outside your door! Stay inside and watch TV!" When we think in concert with human culture, we learn to fear. That fear either muffles our communication, or, if we overreact, it makes us blunt and unloving.

The opposite of fear is not courage; it is love. Jesus says, *"Perfect love casts out all fear."* When we think in more Christ-like ways, we respond to people more often with love. By gaining the mind of Christ, the cure for our fear of approaching young people is to care about them more than we care about our performance or comfort. Love will be the key that unlocks our boldness; wisdom will be the hinge on which it swings open.

27

The Power of Story

"**W**hy do you behave as you do?"

Some folks may brace themselves, expecting to hear some psychological response, but the question is a biblical question from 1 Kings 1. King David's ambitious, but rebellious, son Adonijah is introduced with this strange parenthetical comment: (His father had never interfered with him by asking, "Why do you behave as you do?")

The comment implies that, if someone (in this case, his father) had asked Adonijah the question, the sad trajectory of his life might have changed, but he was not asked and so fell into rebellion, which led to his early death.

Understanding why you behave as you do is important. Seeing the motive and the reasons and setting them beside the truth of our faith helps us heal from wounds, let go of bitterness, and love others better.

Understanding why other people behave as they do is equally important. If we see each other as people without reasons for behaving as we do, even our normal behaviors seem unpredictable and irrational. But when we know a young person's story, where he came from and how he got here, we are more able to extend grace and comfort.

Asking sincerely to hear the life story of a young person makes good things happen. Even if he refuses, he feels wanted. He feels valued. If he tells it, we begin to understand why he behaves as he does. Our fear eases; emotional distance shrinks, and compassion grows.

What would it look like if you asked some young people to tell their stories?

- Trust them to tell you what they can, based on their current trust level with you.
- Listen for early foundations of faith and/or misplaced foundational stones that may block the further building of faith, but don't rush to point them out.
- Listen prayerfully, asking to see the larger story God is drawing with their lives. If God uses our lives to reflect His story, we would be foolish to ignore His reflection in their stories.
- Ask questions to make sure we understand, to clarify what we don't understand, and to demonstrate our genuine interest.
- If their story resonates with something in you or in the Bible, explain it briefly. Don't preach; just offer it as an observation.
- When they are finished with their stories, thank them. Make sure they understand their stories are gifts, that you are honored that they trust you to share them, and that you are grateful for their telling of them.

The Power of Our Stories

If time allows and it seems appropriate, offer to tell your story as well. Give them the honest version with the spiritual parts, the failures, and the triumphs. Use discretion and discernment about what is appropriate to share, but don't be afraid to surprise them with transparency. We are redeemed people. We are not slaves to sin. They may need to see the full measure of grace that we've experienced. If they see your life as a monotonous hum without bumps or dips, they'll have little reason to suspect that you ever needed a relationship with Jesus, or they may decide that Jesus may not be big enough for the mess of their lives.

Consider that the story of King David includes the glorious highs like defeating Goliath and the hideous lows of his immorality with Bathsheba and the death of his sons. Notice the Apostle Paul speaks frankly about his own struggle with the flesh and his sinful past as the "chief of sinners." The listeners don't need to know everything at once, but with young people it may be valuable to set a tone of authenticity rather than glossing over failures to appear more perfect. The parts that we think will damage our reputation may actually build their trust and free them to be more honest. Trust the Holy Spirit to guide you in what to share and in the power of God to redeem even your mistakes.

Invite them to ask questions, and answer their questions honestly. They'll be more likely to answer yours in the future.

28

The Evangelistic Power
of Our Need

There was no one in line, so I introduced myself to the cashier as Scott, a guy from out of town who was working with a local church to help the congregation more effectively reach the young people in their community.

"Can you help me?"

She looked at me for a second, then she shrugged. I took it as a yes and asked her if she'd ever heard of the church I was working with.

"I've driven past it, but I don't go to church. Churches brainwash people."

"Wow. Tell me about that." I set my bag on the counter. She seemed pleased that I wanted to listen.

"I mean, there's only one God right?"

"Right," I agreed.

"So why are there so many different churches? And—"

Then a voice behind me. "I'm sorry...are you talking about my church?"

I turned around and saw a bright-eyed grandmother with bags in hand.

I told her the name of the church.

"It's a good church. I've been there for more than 50

years," she declared. "You should come and see for yourself." She directed it at me in a way that made me expect her to add, "you little whippersnapper!"

But she didn't.

As I started to explain that I was going to be there for the rest of the week, she turned on the cashier. "You should come, too!"

The cashier crossed her arms and stiffened. She repeated her earlier claim, a little harder this time, "Churches brainwash people."

The older lady declared, "Well, you need the Lord."

The cashier blushed and snapped, "I don't want to be preached at," and busied herself at her register.

The older lady shrugged and left the store.

The cashier was done talking. She looked at me with a raised eyebrow that said, "See what I mean?"

"Thanks for taking time to talk. I'm sorry that I put you in that position."

I hurried out of the store and spotted the church lady making her way to a white Toyota way out in the lot. I started running, wondering why a woman her age would park so far out when there were spaces so much closer, but there I went—tall, goofy, bald man swinging my plastic Goody's bag containing black socks and what my daughter calls an "old-man shirt." I'm calling after her, "Ma'am! Ma'am!"

She turned before she got to her car, not sure if I was a friend or an enemy. I slowed and tried to look friendly and harmless.

When I got to her, she looked up at me, "Did I say the wrong thing back there?"

"You told her the truth, but she didn't trust that it was the truth."

I introduced myself and explained my visit to her

church. For the next 40 minutes, we had a delightful talk there in the parking lot. She told me about her life, the church, the loss of her husband, and her sadness to go home to an empty house, despite her assurance that Jesus was with her.

At one point, as we talked about some frustrations she had years ago with some of the members at the church, she said, "It's like they were brainwashed."

She stopped. Realizing what she said, she looked up at me with a twinkle in her eye, and we laughed. Then she turned thoughtful.

"So what should I have said to her?" she wondered, looking back at the store.

At the time I don't think I answered her very well, but later it was so clear. Here is a woman who is faithful and wise but terribly lonely, and a young woman who's never really experienced the love of Christ. Maybe instead of saying, "You need the Lord" to the people we meet, it would be wise to imitate Christ in His encounter with the Samaritan woman at the well. In that moment, Jesus started with **His** need—"I'm thirsty. Can you give Me some water?" but in the end, she was the one who got Living Water. To give people what they really need, sometimes we must start with our need.

Perhaps this older woman could have said to the cashier, "I've been lonely since my husband died. Will you have dinner with me on Monday? You could bring a friend."

And others could say, "I'd like to find some purpose in life since I retired. May I teach you what I know about faith, business, or life?"

Or any of these:

"I'm weak. Will you help me clean up my yard?"

"I'm short! Will you dust the tops of my shelves?"

"I miss having a house full of people! Will you bring some friends over to watch some TV? I'll make dinner!"

"I need help with my computer; could you fix it or teach me to use it well?"

"I need help repairing my car; can you be my helper?"

"My front porch needs painting. Could I pay you to do it?"

"I have some heavy items that need moving. Can you help me?"

I suspect the best missionaries are those who come into a community like children or babies, needing to learn everything—how to get food, how to talk, and how to act in the culture. When missionaries show up telling the indigenous people what they need, they may sound arrogant and the hearers may grow defensive. We may be most effective when we remember yet again, "*His strength is made perfect in our weakness.*"

28

Going Out Right

Many churches are attempting to become more "missional." The addition of missional activity, that which moves us toward individuals in the community, is potentially a glorious change for many churches and individuals. Regrettably, congregants may go zealously with a new picture in their minds and fire in their bellies, but without the heart of Christ behind it. They may sound like this:

"Hey! Look to me, you pitiful sinners! See me moving down to you? Notice that I'm being just like Jesus to you, coming down to you in this filthy place you call a life. But fear not! I am here to rescue you and to free you from the chains that have made you a slave to sin! Because of my love and effort, you must respond well to me."

Do I need to say that this is not the attitude reflective of the mind of Christ? Rather than laying down our lives, we may sound like we are laying down the law. In free nations, much of what the Church calls persecution is the natural response of normal people to our arrogance and our willingness to speak from positions of power, rather than positions of servanthood.

Our new picture of the Gospel should press us, not simply toward people, but toward the imitation of Christ as Paul described in Philippians 2. The prevailing attitude there is humility, but humility to a degree that I'm still hoping for (and terrified of) in my own life.

Clearly, we don't wait for the perfection of our attitude before we move toward the sinner in love; but we must remember that we are still reluctant to make ourselves nothing, and reluctant to empty ourselves. Admitting that reluctance to ourselves and to God is healthy and wise. Admitting it to others allows them to look past our mistakes or blind spots to see the reflection of Christ more clearly in our movement toward them.

There is a great deal of talk about the Truth and/or Biblical worldview among church folks. My experience has been that many of those who talk about them forget that the foundation of Truth and the Bible is the love of God. If Truth is something we use to fight against other people, then it may not be the truth. If our biblical worldview sets us in opposition to the lost, then it may not be a Christian worldview.

The Truth is, we who deserved death have been adopted by grace into the family of God. Consequently, we are called to adopt others into the family of God, not to make sure they know we are right. Again, I am not devaluing the Truth and knowledge of the Bible, but I refuse to promote Truth above love. I would argue the Truth of God cannot be communicated or even exist apart from love.

29

Hospitality:
An Undervalued Ministry

Offer hospitality to one another without grumbling.

(1 Peter 4:9)

There are ministries that are more glamorous and exciting than hospitality, but in a culture where young people hope for a place that feels like home, it may be time to honor this ministry more highly in the Body.

The Legacy of Hospitable Couples

When I talk to adult Christians about their faith development, I often hear of hospitable couples who invested in young people's faith: small group leaders, Bible study leaders, or just gracious couples.

For instance, John and LaRose Allman started as Wise Guides. Eventually they became spiritual parents to dozens of young people who flowed through their home over the years. I interviewed some of them. Each agreed that the time they spent in the home of John and LaRose was a significant factor in their development as lifelong disciples.

The fruit of the Allmans' lives was multiplied in young people who now lead families, churches, ministries and businesses. It multiplied into their marriages, which are stronger because they saw the Allmans working together, serving one another, and reflecting Jesus every week in a strong marriage. For those who grew up with single parents, that picture of a strong marriage gave them a vision of what their marriage could be, plus a picture of Christ's love for the Church.

Growing up in Charlotte, I saw the love of Christ in Tip and Pat Johnson, another couple who opened their home to young people each week for years. Sometimes the group that met in their home planned outings together, but the basis of the group was regular time in the home of a mature and wonderfully warm husband and wife who loved each other dearly and let the overflow of their lives in Christ spill out generously onto others.

My wife Michele lived with some Wise Guides when she was in college. She stunned Lewis and Melissa Young when she announced over dinner that she didn't believe in hell, but the Youngs responded with wisdom, grace, and love. They didn't argue or scold her. They had a discussion. They asked questions to figure out why she believed what she believed. They discipled her in the faith. Better than that, they parented her in the faith.

Later Gally and Fielding Gallivan opened their home to Michele. They just loved her. They trusted her to watch over their boys. For her, their faith, warmth, and steadiness made living in their home like living in a safe hug. They became her family. Gally even walked her down the aisle when we were married.

As I started this book, I met with a graduate of my youth ministry. She had wanted to talk to me for a while and when we finally got together, she said something very close to this: "First of all, I need to thank you. Not for all the teaching you did or the youth-pastor stuff you did, but for letting me stay overnight at your home so often. It was really important. When I was in counseling recently, trying to heal from being sexually abused for years, the counselor asked me when I felt safe while I was growing up, and I said it was the times I spent the night at your home."

After I got over the shock and guilt of not protecting her more, I told her she was always welcome, but honestly, she should thank the Gallivans, the Youngs, and the Johnsons. Those couples taught Michele and me that hospitality is an important ministry, that opening your home to welcome the stranger as family is valuable in ways we don't immediately understand.

What would it look like if you opened your home to some young people for fellowship or Bible study or discussion?

30

A House Divided

Physical Separation

Churches tend to program with a powerful, imaginary grid in place. It organizes ages and needs into ministries and classes. It seems normal for young ones to be in nursery and children's church every week, for youth to be in youth Sunday school or the youth service or the youth group, while their parents go to a parenting class, and the older members go to the Sunday school class they've attended for the last 22 years. We have programs for young mothers, basketball for men, circles for women, Bible studies for divorcees, and young adult ministries for young adults. With this grid in place, each group has its own defined territory, its own resources, its own purpose, and its own line item in the budget. It all feels efficient and effective, but it is effectively dividing and killing the Church.

Emotional Separation

The persistent physical separation of the generations builds a relational barrier, which youth leaders and adult congregations must work hard to disrupt.

Youth Leader Contributions

Rebellion is a powerful motivator in young people, especially those who have been wounded by authority or feel unwanted. No youth pastor I've met would say, "I consciously intended to sow rebellion into my group," but youth ministry leaders (and their volunteers) can build community around a quiet rebellion by simply whispering or agreeing, "Our youth group is cooler, hipper, hotter, louder, and/or more spiritual than adult church."

With that perception, the youth group grows with a clear sense of identity, but develops in opposition to the adult community ("big church"), which becomes the bad guy. The youth group identifies with David, the young anointed one, being taunted by the Goliath of the big, old church. In this case, if the youth group's identity is built as a reaction against the adult church, no self-respecting young person would dare grow up wanting to leave David to join Goliath.

I saw the damage of pitting students against "big church" in my first ministry job. An angry student approached me to complain that the adult worship team had used one of "our (youth-group) songs in big church without permission."

I gently explained the danger of his attitude, but confessed to him, and later the whole group, that I had contributed to those feelings and that we needed to end that picture of the territorial grid. We all shared a "teachable moment," and soon the group was delighted to share their songs and their talents with the adult church.

Division can happen pretty innocently. For example, when the church staff or adults make a legitimate complaint to the youth pastor, for instance, about the mess the group left in a room, a youth pastor can inadvertently protect himself from responsibility while shifting grumpiness onto the adult church with a statement to his group, like, "Hey guys, I got some complaints from adults last week about the condition of the room. Let's make sure that we leave it in better shape this week."

His statement is true, but it subtly positions the adult church as the grumpy complainers. Admittedly, it works to motivate the students to be more diligent, but they clean the room to avoid the disapproval of the adult church. Resentment grows; poison spreads; generations separate.

Alternately, the leader of the same group could own the responsibility of the mess and distribute it to the group, which would sound more like this: "Hey, I let you all get out of here last week without cleaning up. We left a mess. From now on, let's make sure we leave the room better than we found it. I've got sign-up sheets on the wall for student leaders who will handle clean-up teams."

The goal of youth ministry is not to build a wonderful youth group. The goal is to give a good foundation to lifelong disciples who will disciple others. But leaders get tired and look for easy paths. It is easier to find unity in communities when we define the borders more tightly around our little homogeneous group, rather than allowing for a broad range of ages. But if we fail to connect students to the adult church, we undermine their faith development.

Adult Contributions

It is easy to blame youth ministry leaders for the emotional separation, but more often the larger contributor is the adult congregation. Their apathy (or antipathy) toward young people, based on their interactions or avoidances, often poisons the young people toward the adults. Their perception of adults as disapproving or oppressive may be based on their experience. In addition, young people often interpret distance or silence as disapproval. But if adults approach them in love, those assumptions are dispelled.

The wise and loving church will encourage young people to find Wise Guides in their homes or churches. It will call them into adult roles early and build an intergenerational community with programming that is not solely based on age-specific territorialism.

To do that, churches will need to guard the hearts of students from feeling in opposition to the adult church. It's not easy. A pastor told me of the woman in his church who came to her seat and found two young people lingering after the previous service. The woman said to them, "Your service is over. Get out of here."

In that encounter, those two students did not experience the mind of Christ in their church. The older lady owes them an apology. If she does not offer it, those two will require numerous interactions with loving adults in that church to overshadow that encounter and to convince them they are wanted there.

Further, those young people may be immature enough to tell their friends of her offense and the poison spreads. Or the woman may tell her older friends of their disrespect and the divisions widen. At some point someone needs to disrupt that pattern. I place most of the burden on the back of the adult church. We should be the one modeling love and wisdom for the younger ones. We're supposed to be the Wise Guides.

31

One Family

Before you read this book, your role in discipling young people probably meant **getting young people to visit the youth group or some other age-appropriate ministry in the church.**

Having read this far, some might suggest that the new picture in our mind should reflect this: **Discipling young people means adults engage with young people in the youth community, moving them into the adult community in order to experience lifelong faith.**

Certainly that's a step in the right direction. It is a better reaction than just "get them into the youth group," but moving young people into an adult community presumes that there are two communities: one for the child and one for the adult—an un-renewed view of Christian community.

Consider that the typical rite of passage is a movement from the community of children to the community of adults, but Jesus reverses the direction of the passage. Rather than being promoted to a higher level, Christ requires that we be "born again" and declaring that unless we come as a child we will not enter into the Kingdom. Secondly, He dissolves the idea of two communities, pressing us into one family in which we are all adopted sons and daughters of one Father; ***all are*** children and siblings in a single family. A single community.

The rite of passage for the young person in the Church is movement into a new role in the same community or family. He gets more responsibility, more freedom, more input, more trust, and more intentional guidance from the adults in the larger community of faith beyond his parents. In his passage to adulthood, the young person does not leave the younger behind or move above them or distant from them. In other words he does not leave THEM to come to US. He is US, but his role is changing, and we are to help him in that change.

There is little room in orthodox Christian thought for any believers moving to a position above another person or to a position where they can be unconcerned about the needs of another. Our model in Christ is servanthood and humility, not senior privileges and control. We are given authority and influence, not to protect the organization, our office, or ourselves, but to love the people and reflect to all the attitude of Christ Jesus.

Springboard for discussion: What is your attitude toward the young people of your church? Is there any part of you that looks down on them or sees them as separate from the adults?

32

Weaving Generations

In my experience, discipleship happens best in intergenerational relationships in a unified community, or more simply: **Discipleship of young people happens best in churches that function as a loving family.**

Why can't a fifth grader serve on your VBS planning committee?

Why can't a twelve-year-old run your projector?

Why can't you include teens on the pastoral search committee or the missions committee?

Why do you need to have a children's choir and a youth choir? Why not let them all sing with the adult choir?

Why not let children and teens serve on ministry and prayer teams?

Why do you have youth mission trips and adult mission trips? Why can't they go together?

Why can't the high school boys go on the Men's Retreat?

Why can't the children, teens, and young adults be involved in small groups?

Why can't the empty nesters host dinners for the young singles or young couples?

Why can't the generations be together more often?

My point is this: The separation of the generations that we have accepted and designed into our programming is damaging the Church and undermining the very goal we designed our programming to reach.

What about Youth Ministry?

We have pumped billions into staffing and resources for youth and young-adult ministry, yet more often than not, it is failing to create lifelong disciples. In our traditional model of ministry, our earnest efforts have created stark generational divisions within the Church, dropping most of our young people into a relational vacuum after graduation from high school.

I don't believe better or more youth ministry is the solution to the problem of young people leaving the Church, but I am not an opponent of youth ministry. Not at all! Building peer relationships for students is important. Providing opportunities for students to serve and lead is essential. Creating entry points for young people to enter the Church community with peers is valuable. Teaching young people in relevant and practical ways is helpful, but we need to rethink the overall goals, models, and strategies of our youth ministries. We need to build lifelong disciples, rather than great youth and young-adult groups apart from adult relationships in the larger congregation.

Further, our current models are self-limiting in growth. Most youth ministry veterans affirm that a healthy youth group will demonstrate attendance that equals about 10% of the average attendance at worship services in a weekend. With intentional investment youth-group attendance may reach 20% of church attendance, but the ability of that organization to sustain those numbers weakens, until the number falls to a sustainable level below the 20% ceiling.[9]

But if the Church is a family, why are the ratios so low? My children outnumber my wife and me. I know a family with 13 children. Can the children in a church not outnumber the adults? If we are willing to function as family, rather than as an organization, we may be able to rethink the limits and measures we currently use in youth evangelism.

Incremental Weaving

A church that renews its thinking about young people will incrementally weave students and young adults into the fabric of the church. Sudden, large changes by staff or leadership are not necessary and may be unloving and foolish. The significant change must first happen in the hearts of the adult members. Church staff can encourage it. They can adapt their current programming to include a broad range of ages, but unity between the generations will not happen unless the hearts of adults are turned toward the children and the children's to the adults. This takes persistent intentionality and renewed thinking.

One Sunday morning several years ago, I passed five women, who sat in the same section every Sunday morning.

"Good morning, ladies!"

"What's all this?" one asked, skipping the cheery "good morning" they usually offered. They were all eyeing

---

[9] DeVries, M. (2008). *Sustainable Youth Ministry: Why Most Youth Ministry Doesn't Last and What Your Church Can Do about It.* InterVarsity Press.

the students tuning their guitars and warming up on the stage before the service.

"It's Youth Sunday!" I was so excited it burst out of me.

It was our first official Youth Sunday during my tenure there. I was to preach my first sermon. It was about loving one another. The youth handled everything else. They decorated the church inside and out. They had designed a special bulletin. They would handle the music, parking lot duties, the greeting out front, the announcements, the soundboard, the cameras, and the lights. They would dance, sing, and do dramas. They even stood on the street out front, like we were having a car wash, beckoning cars to turn in and join us for services, and people did turn in.

Everyone involved was so excited, but these older ladies were not. They looked knowingly at each other, gathered their Bibles and purses, stood up, and moved as a group to the back row, mumbling about the noise and the fuss.

Honestly, I was miffed. Clearly we weren't loving each other very well just then.

Fast forward three years: Youth Sunday again. Five widows sitting in their regular seats.

"Good morning, ladies!" I said, a little cautiously.

"It's Youth Sunday!" one of them gushed.

"Yes, it is!" I replied.

They started chattering like middle-schoolers. "Oh, we've been looking forward to this!"

"It's our favorite service of the year."

"We really should do it more often."

They were absolutely giddy. What happened in three years?

Lots.

At the first Youth Sunday, expectations were low. The adults suspected it would be too loud and the songs would be completely different. They expected the kids to take over the service and demonstrate how they wanted the service to be, but the students had determined that their job was to lead the service for everyone, not force their worship on the adults. They must do what was loving and best for the "family," not necessarily what they wanted to do. Not to prove what they could do, but to love well.

So the youth played hymns and familiar songs and introduced a couple of new ones at normal volumes. The students prayed over adults at the end of the service. They did everything with excellence and joy. The results were stunning. There was a quiet awe in the adults at what the young people offered. It felt like a gift from the students to the adult church, and the lesson for all of us was powerful.

The second year built on that first year. It went equally as well. By the third year, the lines were blurry. The students were already part of the normal adult worship band. They were running the lights, computers, the sound, and the video cameras in every service. They were part of the greeting team, the ushers, and the ministry teams.

Youth Sunday was the big visible lever that we used to move the generations closer, but the move was also a product of small, persistent decisions by the entire staff to incrementally weave young people into the fabric of the adult church, like encouraging high school girls to attend the women's ministry events or sending upperclassmen to adult Sunday School classes. Lots of little things like that connected the congregation and the students. Kids felt wanted and trusted. Adults felt more comfortable approaching them. Older members eventually became spiritual parents for kids who needed them. The whole place became a little more like the family we really are. That sense of family drew more students hungry for what their friends had.

However, *the primary solution to reaching and keeping young people does not lie in programming decisions made by church staff*. The solution is adults just like you moving toward young people in love with renewed hearts and minds. A church staff can encourage, but the real impact happens between individuals, not in organizations. Hopefully, churches have organizational systems that promote the weaving of the generations, and individuals willing to be woven together, but once students are woven into an intergenerational community that loves them well, they bring their friends, and they don't wander away from it easily, and mature members notice if they do.

33

A Collection of "What Ifs"

What if you invited a young person to sit with you or your family during a service and then invited him to lunch after church? What if you asked to hear his life story once you got there?

What if you asked a young person and a friend in your church to go to lunch with you during the week?

What if you introduced yourself to the young people who spend time in the street outside your home?

What if you made them cookies or offered them iced tea or hot chocolate (depending on the weather)?

What if you adopted a college student and prayed for him, encouraged him with calls, and sent letters, exam survival kits, and care packages?

What if you loved someone well today by moving out of your safe place or routine and toward him? You don't have to know what to do when you get there. Just say, "I'm reading a book that told me to move toward someone I love. I thought of you and so here I am! I don't know what to do now. Is there anything you need?"

Watch their responses.

What if your small group broke into three sub-groups for 13 weeks to provide a class, group, or activity for a group of younger people in the church? At the end of

13 weeks, what if you have a big cookout for all those who participated and share stories of what you learned?

What if the men of your men's ministry adopted a local school and mentored the most high-risk students in that school? What would the impact be on the community in five years?

What if the youth ministry of your church quit meeting for eight weeks and used that time to interview, videotape, edit, and post online the testimonies and life stories of the older saints in your church? **What if** they sent the link to their favorite video to their friends at school when they were finished?

What if God asked you, like He asked Moses, "What's in your hand?" What resources, knowledge, skills, connections, or time do you have that God might use to build discipling relationships? Here are a few ideas:

Resources	Skills	Interests
A boat on a lake	Art	Camping
Sporting equipment	Music	History
Season Tickets	Home repair	Politics
TV	Auto repair	Sports
Tools	Cooking	Music
Money	Carpentry	Business
Musical Instruments	Knitting	The Bible
A big yard	Scrapbooking	Movies
A grill	Parenting	Television
A house	Dog-training	

What if you invited young people over to watch their favorite show with your family? **What if** you provided coffee and light snacks and conversation before/after the show? **What if** at the end of the season you invited them to keep coming over to discuss topics that are important to them?

What if two or three wise, bold, but humble saints with faith that God will use them on the spot sat in the mall, in a park, or next to a college campus with shirts or signs that said "We offer free wisdom"? When the young people come and ask a question, even a mocking one like, "What's the meaning of life?" these saints would look past the mocking to the heart of the individual. They would pray briefly and then ask questions of the young person to learn more, and then, if appropriate, offer them biblical advice or next steps. Perhaps they would exchange phone numbers or email addresses or commit to be in the same spot at the same time next week, and build relationships from there.

What if you ask a young couple to join you and your spouse for lunch or to go to a movie and get coffee afterwards?

What if a shy person teamed with a talkative person who would do all the talking, so the introvert could do whatever he is good at behind the scenes in building a discipling group in a home?

What if you ask two or three unchurched young people to lunch or dinner where you ask for their help? Explain you are reading a book that told you to have them draw out their picture of what they think Christianity is about, who Jesus is, and what He did. (Don't presume they know what "Gospel" means.) Listen well without interrupting or correcting. Ask questions for clarifying only.

When they are finished, thank them. Explain that the book you are reading offers two different pictures of the Gospel. Draw and explain them both. Ask them to stop you if you use words or phrases they don't understand. When you finish, ask them some questions.

"Were any parts of this unclear to you?"

"Did anything I say surprise you or confuse you?"

"Which picture makes more sense?"

"Any other thoughts?"

34

Closing

In the first pages of this book, we left Mr. Harding and David sitting silently beside each other, blind to the opportunity that God had orchestrated in getting them together—the younger one driven there by the turmoil of his family, the older one unmoved from the same comfortable spot for 30 years. Now their lives awkwardly bump together and then apart by a few feet, and they sit in silence, separated by their fear and their old ways of thinking.

Mr. Harding's life has been disrupted. He can let inertia settle him into his resting state, quietly embarrassed by his petty demand for his seat, or he can surf the wave of opportunity that rolled through his pew. If he chooses to surf it, what should Mr. Harding do?

Again, there is no formula for this, beyond "love well and walk by faith," but let me give you a narrative of what could happen, just to let you see Wise Guides in action.

Here's how it might go for Mr. Harding:

Prayerful Assessment

His first steps are internal. Mr. Harding will need to prayerfully assess some things:

What is God doing here in this moment? Why am I behaving as I am? Is it fear? Irritation? Selfishness? Or something else?

Can I be a Wise Guide to this young man?

If Mr. Harding's already swamped, he'll feel less than motivated to take on another relationship, but if he has room to be a Wise Guide, he'll have to pray for wisdom, grace, and love for this young man. Then he may pray specifically for him. He'll remember that any good effects will not come from his cleverness or his skill, but from the Lord. Prayer will be essential.

Recognition and Preparation

Mr. Harding will also need to recognize some thoughts and prepare emotionally:

- "My perception of this young man as a foreigner intruding on my territory is not reflective of the mind of Christ. I need to picture him as an Orphan in need of a Wise Guide. He needs me to interrupt the drudgery of his life."

- "I need to expect that this young man may respond poorly at first. Rather than take it personally, I will prepare to see it as a defense that he has learned, and being wiser, I'll be prepared to parry the move and move closer in safe ways."

Harding must recognize that David needs a relationship with Christ, but will not presume that he does or does not have one. If David does not have faith, it may not spring up immediately. David may need to experience the love of Christ individually and through a new loving community/family before he believes. He may need to see the reflection of Christ in Mr. Harding and the community around him. So this morning, Harding's goal is to move toward David in love, not get him saved and be done with him.

Approach

Now the first outward things happen: In his own style, Mr. Harding would introduce himself and learn David's name. Then he would apologize and explain the whole "my seat" comment from earlier. In the process, he would explain a bit about his family who sat with him here for so long, and then add that there's plenty of room now for David to sit here.

That would be a natural lead-in to asking about David. Why he was there? Was he waiting for someone else? Who invited him? What was he going to do later in the day? David would most likely answer with grunts and nods and short answers. Mr. Harding would recognize that his responses are not rooted in disrespect but in fear.

Support/Equip

Once the service started, Mr. Harding would guide him through the service and share a bulletin or hymnal where appropriate. This might build trust.

Connect Him to a Community

Then, if he wanted, he'd figure out if David had any plans or responsibilities after lunch. If David had none, he'd nearly insist that David go to lunch with him and his friends, his treat. David would refuse, but Mr. Harding would persist in appropriate ways (calming fears, addressing objections) until David relented.

Protect/Provide

He'd ride to lunch with David and a friend to protect them both and to ease the tension of this first meeting.

Along the way, Mr. Harding would assure David he was delighted that he came and that he understands it may seem odd, but that he prayed about it, and it seemed like he was supposed to invite him along. He'd reassure David that he's safe and that the people at lunch will be safe as well, though if there are characters who are less than safe, Mr. Harding will tell David about them while assuring David that he'll guard him.

Building Rapport/Trust

If appropriate, he'd ask to hear David's story at lunch. He'd ask appropriate questions about what David offers. In the confusing spots, where David seemed guarded or vague, he'd ask questions, like, "Can you help me understand this part of your story? It seemed blurry to me. If you meant it to be blurry, I understand. We can skip it if you'd rather."

He'd ask questions about David's school, his activities, hobbies, and what he thought of the church service. He'd respond authentically to all he heard, but remind himself that he's not trying to fix David. If appropriate, Mr. Harding would tell David his story, or part of it.

His goal is to build a safe foundation of trust. With an eye toward David's future as a lifelong disciple, Mr. Harding is not in a panic to "get him saved," but he does not avoid talk of spiritual things.

Make Him Wanted/Needed/Trusted

As lunch ends, he'd ask people at the table if David was welcome next week. Hopefully, they'd agree, and David would be formally invited to join them again next week. After taking David back to the church with the same friend in the car, Mr. Harding might get an email or a phone number from David, and ask permission to contact him if he needs help during the week with a project he has planned.

If that need arose, Mr. Harding would contact him and ask him to come over at a specific time or go get him as scheduled. Then they'd work together. The goal is building relationship and trust, so he'd feel free to demonstrate his trust of David leaving him with the job and going elsewhere for a bit. Mr. Harding would be encouraging, instructive, and corrective where appropriate.

As David leaves, Mr. Harding makes sure David feels wanted. Perhaps he says something like, "I'll save your seat for you on Sunday. I hope to see you there. The group is expecting you at lunch. We'll miss you if you're not there."

If David does not show up, Mr. Harding calls him after the service, before he goes to lunch. He knows that anytime a kid's cell phone rings, it means someone cares. He offers to stop by and pick him up.

It may be wise for Mr. Harding to express his own needs as well, "I don't like sitting alone in church, and I enjoyed sitting with you."

Connect Him to a New Identity and a New Power

Along the way, he'll be looking for the cracks that God placed in David's heart to let in truth and love, but if David refuses to talk of spiritual things, Harding may look for other questions like, "What do you want to learn how to do? What skill or knowledge do I have that you need? What are you interested in or really good at?"

Harding may offer a list of what he knows about (physical work/sports, relational skills, educational skills, and spiritual things), the activities he's involved in, hobbies he enjoys, and the things he's willing to learn about with David.

If David says, "I don't know." Or "nuthin,'" Mr. Harding is not discouraged; he hears the answer, not as apathy or lack of ambition, but as fear that grips David like death and stops him from taking risks. Mr. Harding gets to play the Hero, the Samson, who comes to find the honey in that death, so he leaves the invitation open, saying, "Let me know when you figure it out. I'd be glad to help."

At some point, David will have a question about the sermon or the service or something Mr. Harding says. That will make an easy lead-in to asking what he knows currently about Jesus and spiritual things. It may happen the first week or it could be four years.

Modeling Values

Mr. Harding would be wise to engage David's parents, to reassure them and to dignify their role in his life. He's not trying to steal their child; he's trying to help him. David's parents may not be perfect, but they are not the enemy. He'll not be naïve, but he'll do nothing to discredit them or feed David's anger toward them. He'll urge David to understand that his stepfather behaves as he does for reasons, while asking David why he behaves as he does.

If the parents set boundaries or limits, Mr. Harding would model his value of authority with the acknowledgement of David's parents' authority and adhere to their rules fully and cheerfully.

If David has no boundaries or limits, Mr. Harding would set his own to protect David and enforce them without fail.

Guiding, Not Controlling

Mr. Harding would remember that he is not building a dependent, but a young man to be released into adulthood. He is not controlling or manipulative with guilt or shame. He does not fake his moods or his patience with David. He is authentic and treats David as a young man, not a child.

If David makes a bad choice, Mr. Harding does not rescue him from natural consequences and does not withdraw relationship as punishment, though he is clear about boundaries and expectations of behavior if David expects him to stay engaged. If David persistently violates those boundaries, Mr. Harding will end the relationship for a season, making sure that David knows it would restart the moment he returns repentant.

Despite his efforts to build trust, if David threatens to hurt himself or someone else, Mr. Harding would inform the appropriate people (parents, pastor, etc.).

Pressing Through Conflict

At some point, either David or Mr. Harding will make a mistake. One or both will be offended or hurt. Mr. Harding will know that this relationship has reached a new opportunity. He will model loving confrontation and/or confession. He'll speak the truth in love, confessing his error and/or confronting David's. His goal is restored relationship, not ignored tension. They'll work it out and end up better off than before.

Then?

Mr. Harding and David will know what to do next. This is not a formula or a program It is a discipling relationship. It may turn out more formal with a specific meeting time. It may turn out very informal. It may just be eight months of fluffy talk if David is too wounded to trust quickly. It may end if David can't or won't trust him, but if it continues, at some point it will go deeper.

Eventually David may invite friends and, on Tuesday nights, Mr. Harding may have a living room full of David's friends watching movies and eating pizza at his home. He may invite a trusted friend over to help him. Over time the group's discussions will turn to deeper life issues and spiritual matters, but Mr. Harding knows he needs to be patient.

In the end, the trajectory of lives will be changed, because Mr. Harding's seat got taken, and he decided to leave his safe place and move toward a young person as a Wise Guide, hoping to imitate Jesus as he did.

Today, it's our turn. What might it look like for you?

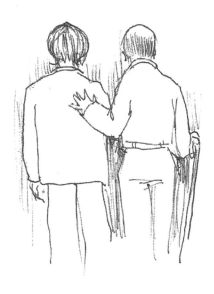

Sharing Your Stories, Questions

Please know that I am grateful for your time and energy in reading this far. I pray it was worth it.

Since we are family in Christ, I invite you to go to scottwilcher.com and share ideas and stories of your efforts (and failures) or questions as a Wise Guide and Spiritual Parent to reflect the love and humility of Christ in your movement toward the young people around you.

Or offer a tribute to a Wise Guide who reflected Christ to you.

Or ask questions about what to do next.

The UpStream Project

A 501c3 non-profit that helps aging churches reach and keep the next generation. For more information, see our website at scottwilcher.com.

Appendix

Solo Guiding: A Warning

I am not naïve. I know that intergenerational relationships can go horribly wrong. I just watched one of my former students (not the one who stayed at my home) face the agony of the second trial in the second state of the same man who molested her repeatedly from the age of six on. Though I have only seen slivers of the damage he caused in her life, her relationships, and her family, it breaks my heart.

If I were the enemy of the Church and wanted to destroy a generation, I would wreck their families first, and then isolate them from wise adults by undermining their ability to trust.

In the Catholic Church, the failure to deal with the priests who molested children has damaged the reputation of the entire Church and the confidence of the public regarding all church leaders.

Though research statistics on the frequency of sexual abuse vary, most studies suggest that 1 in 4 women and 1 in 7 men have been sexually abused. The question we all ask is, "Who can we trust?" More appropriately, our question as Wise Guides should be, "Can they trust me?"

If the answer is anything less than a triumphant "yes," we must reexamine our involvement in the role. We must discern if we are moving toward our disciples to fulfill our own appetites, or if we are moving toward them in purity and love to equip them and to launch them toward their destinies.

I beg you: Don't be part of the damage.

- Assume you are weak and vulnerable to temptation.
- Put boundaries and safeguards in place. Do not depart from them.
- Work with other adults in teams or pairs, whenever possible.
- Have individuals hold you accountable to purity and wise ministry practices.
- If you are tempted or feeling weak, end the discipling relationship. It is better that a young person experience confusion and rejection than the trauma of sexual abuse.

If there is any question about your safety as a discipler, talk with your pastor before you move toward anyone with the intent of being a Wise Guide. If your pastor denies you the right to disciple or simply suggests that you not do it, accept the decision and submit to his authority and wisdom without question. In the coming months and years, do all you can to rebuild your character and repair the trust of the community.

Taking offense at his decision, going to a different church, or complaining about the decision will simply reveal that you are not ready to disciple someone else in healthy ways. You would sow your rebellion into that follower. We're supposed to be Wise Guides, not Selfish Fools.

But if your heart is pure, and God provides opportunity—go! Move toward them. Others will join in eventually.

Acknowledgements

By earthly standards, I am not a rich man, but I have a huge treasure of relationships in my family and friends. I am grateful to God for them all. Some folks deserve special thanks for their contributions to this book:

The many youth, young adults, and volunteers who shared their lives with me.

Lori, who cheerfully handles the details so I don't have to.

Brent, Walt, Paul, Gil, Mike, Brad, Barry, and Dave for their wisdom and friendship.

My supporters, who invested in my vision, even when it seemed blurry.

The staff and people of KPC in Virginia Beach and St. Giles Presbyterian in Charlotte for your trust, patience, and laughter when I tried new tactics in youth ministry.

Angus for friendship, encouragement, and goading.

Roy, who asks great questions that need asking.

Pastors Don Neighbors, Keith Cobb, John Dooley, Marty O'Rourke, and Jim Brown—who offered kindness and trust when I started this ministry and extended great grace as I learned.

To my Wise Guides: French O'Shields, John Brown, Gally Gallivan, Percy Burns, Gerry Edwards, Bud Carrier, Hal Uzzel, and Charles Deal.

My prayer warriors all over the world.

My mom, Ann Wilcher, for the illustrations and so much more.

Leslie, Lauren and Michael, for your generosity in sharing me with everyone else's children.

With special recognition of Evelyn Wagoner and Pam Piccolo, my writing gurus and editors for their time, talent, and energy to get this book to print.

Thanks,

About the Author

Rev. Scott Wilcher is passionate about keeping young people as lifelong disciples of Jesus Christ. He has worked with young people and their families his entire adult life.

As founder and executive director of *The UpStream Project*, a ministry researching issues surrounding youth and young adult ministry, Scott is pressing for worldwide reformation of traditional models of youth ministry that is failing to keep young people connected and active in their faith communities. He teaches churches to connect young people with adult congregations in discipling relationships. He also trains youth-ministry teams and advises church leaders on youth and young adult ministry. As part of the National Network of Youth Ministries, Scott facilitates regular meetings to equip and encourage youth pastors.

His articles on youth ministry and leadership have appeared in *Group Magazine*, *Youth Leaders Only*, and other national publications. He is also working toward a doctorate in Strategic Leadership at Regent University.

Scott is married to Michele and has three children, Leslie, Lauren, and Michael.

Coming soon: Scott's upcoming book will address the need for renewed thinking about our individual identities and relationships.

For more information about resources and services for your church, contact scottwilcher@gmail.com.